Young Peoples Story of the Creation

BALBIR SANDHU

ISBN (Paperback): 978-1-958082-87-4

ISBN (Ebook): 978-1-958082-88-1

Printed in the United States of America

DEDICATED TO:
Mom and Dad

CONTENTS

LIST OF ILLUSTRATIONS

LIST OF TABLES

FOREWORD

TO THE TEACHER

This book is not a substitute for a traditional textbook for American high school students but is written to be a supplemental reading. It is assumed that a regular science book is assigned to the class for the detailed treatment of the subject. This book is written in a condensed form, arranging the unified topics in such a sequence to help the student grasp the basics of the subject. The writer, by training, has work experience and exposure to basically all areas of science that bear on everyday life and has treated only the descriptive aspect of science and has left out the mathematics. Review exercises for examination questions generally provided in a traditional textbook are omitted, leaving it to the instructor to develop such exercises.

TO THE STUDENT

This book is intended to be a supplementary reading material in addition to the standard textbook assigned to your level of the class. Because this book does not cover a detailed treatment and mathematical topics, it is more of an inspirational reading than a textbook.

Whether you will be a science-major student in college or will pursue a liberal arts career, this book will help you know your aptitude and aspirations. Starting with the basics of astronomy—the galaxies, the solar system, and the planets—the subjects of science are explored in the succeeding chapters. A concise history of mankind from the beginning to the present is discussed in the concluding chapter of "Life on Earth." Thus, the book will serve as a motivational tool for science-oriented students and offers the basics of social studies for liberal arts students. The career fields open to science-major students are listed. The areas are very wide—from astronomy to aeronautical engineering, chemistry to chemical engineering, geology to petroleum engineering, plant life to agriculture, and life sciences to medicine. In fact, you can pick and choose what you want to do in life and enjoy doing it. This little book will help you explore whatever you enjoy the most and will help you succeed in it. The enjoyment and the success feed each other. I hope you enjoy this book.

ACKNOWLEDGMENTS

The first and foremost credit for the thought of this book goes to my dear friend, William H. Herrin, who first introduced me to the Bible, leading me to insights on the science of creation. This book is therefore the result of years of growth initiated by Bill.

Also, for the encouragement and advice of Sue Bradbury, editor-in-chief of the Folio Society in London, England, I am much grateful. I received these pieces of advice in the form of long and encouraging letters over a period of several years.

I am especially thankful to my friends and office colleagues Phillip French and Brian Bergdall for offering valuable suggestions. Finally this book became a reality only with the timely help of Shauna Gonzales for typing, editing, and arranging the material with the illustrations—a job that needed a lot of patience and skill.

The patience and moral support of my wife, Kulwant, is greatly appreciated for allowing me endless hours, days, and months in seclusion to work on this book—a seclusion utmost necessary for intense thinking.

As this book is a science book with biblical content, I am greatly thankful for the encouragement, spiritual growth, and inspiration I received from my Christian friends, enabling me to stay on course.

CHAPTER 1

INTRODUCTION

GOALS AND OBJECTIVES

There are several reasons to move a writer to attempt the story of the creation for young people of high school age.

The first and foremost reason for this motivation is to present to the young people the basics of the science of creation, which includes astronomy, physics, geology, chemistry, and biology. The presentations are based on established laws of science. On reading H. G. Wells's book The Outline of History and Charles Darwin's books on modifications of species of animals and plants, it is noteworthy that the authors of these books have presented the viewpoints of a select group of scientists about the origins of life on Earth based on observations of plants, insects, birds, and small animals in the first half of the nineteenth century. The observed findings are then extrapolated to geological timescale as a speculative conjecture without sound scientific basis. Correcting the existing deficiencies of the science curriculum of high schools is the primary goal of this book.

Another important goal the writer has in mind is to expose the young minds to practically all areas of science in the early years of education so that they themselves can choose for which particular branch they have the aptitude to pursue in college-level studies.

The third and most important goal of this book is to present science as a fun subject and not a dry, dull topic as most nonscience-major students perceive. A student achieves high standing in a subject that he or she enjoys most. It is the writer's goal to provide necessary motivation and inspiration to science students to achieve higher learning in college and to succeed in their chosen career field.

In chapter 2, the reader is given a concise description of the universe dealing with the stars, outer galaxies, and our own Milky Way galaxy. Also, a brief reference is made to the astronomers who devoted their lifetimes in studying the heavenly bodies using their improved telescopes and new methods of discovery. The name of Edwin Hubble, a brilliant American astronomer, stands out among the world's leading astronomers of the twentieth century along with the names of European Renaissance astronomers. Lastly, the name of Albert Einstein and his theory of relativity stand out in the history of modern science.

Chapters 3 and 4 are devoted to the presentation of our solar system, our Sun being one of the stars in our Milky Way galaxy and closest to Earth. Since our Sun has a direct bearing on our lives and our well-being, we know more about it than we know of any other heavenly body. A brief description of the Sun and a summary of its data are given. The Moon, with its beautiful light and shining delight, is briefly described. We know a great deal more about it after the first American Moon landing by NASA's spacecraft Apollo 11 in the year 1969.

Chapters 5 and 6 are devoted to our home planet, Earth. Chapter 5 is fully devoted to the sciences of physics and chemistry, and chapter 6, to geology and mineralogy. Within the last century, a great deal is known about Earth's crust, geology, mineral resources, and interior. Since these topics are of great interest to science-major students, all its aspects are fully narrated without mathematical treatment. For example, Newton's laws of motion and laws of gravitation are briefly described.

A very brief discussion of the contributions of various famous scientists is given. The names of Polish Nicolaus Copernicus, German Johannes Kepler, Italian Galileo Galilei, and English Isaac Newton stand out in the history of the science of creation. The discussion starts with chemical composition of Earth, the 103 elements, and the many chemical compounds.

Chapter 7 deals with the four stages of life on Earth starting with vegetation, then sea creatures and land creature, and finally, the appearance of man and woman.

Chapter 8 presents the subject of the classification of all living beings into kingdoms; and each kingdom into classes, orders, families, and genera; and finally, into species in accordance with international scientific scheme. This specialty of biology is called taxonomy.

Theories on the origins of life put forth by various scientists are discussed in chapter 9. Scientists believe that while orbiting the Sun, molten masses of Earth started cooling and the crust was formed. Heat, light, and the Sun's ultraviolet radiation bathed Earth. Years and years of condensation of water formed the oceans. Organic compounds were formed in hot oceans where the miracle of life in the form of cyanobacteria emerged. Then in accordance with Darwin's theory, the process of evolution started and resulted in species of plants, animals, and humans. However speculative these theories seem, many scientists believe in them.

In the recent past, with the advances in life sciences and the advent of electron microscopes with magnifying power of fifty thousand, the beliefs in old theories are shaken. Because of many unanswered questions by old theories, there arose a widespread opposition to the theory of evolution. A thorough discussion of Charles Darwin's theory is presented, listing some of the unanswered questions. Chapter 10 gives overview of chapters 7, 8, and 9, elaborating the main points and conclusions.

Finally, a list of bibliographic references is provided for students interested in pursuing additional reading.

CHAPTER 2

THE UNIVERSE

The splendor of the star-filled night sky observed on a moonless night and far away from any city light is a breathtaking panorama the beauty of which no artist's brush or poet's words can express. For thousands of years, people have looked up at the heavens and wondered and contemplated the nature of the universe. Just like our ancestors, we find ourselves asking the same questions, such as the following: How was the universe created? Where did Earth, Moon, and Sun come from? What are stars made of? What is our role in the cosmic and greater scheme of things? This curiosity and the characteristic of our mind to explore and discover is the unique quality that distinguishes us from all other creatures that make up over a million species now inhabiting Earth. Further, it is our unique characteristic to ponder over the supreme power of the Almighty Creator in accordance with His laws and His will.

To the ancients, the universe was an awe-inspiring mystery, but it is not so anymore. A part of the universe is visible to the naked eye, a part of it is explored with the aid of high-powered telescopes and modern space explorations, and a large part is still unknown and unexplored. Though many mysteries of the universe have been gradually revealed to us over a long period of time starting with the ancients and continued with the brilliant works of Copernicus, Kepler, Galileo, Newton, and Einstein, its vastness and extent is still a mystery. On the other hand, whatever has been explored so far, we are very certain about it because of the power of mathematics and science, which are our tools for gaining this knowledge. Whatever is beyond our knowledge, we can only guess, and this remains the subject of future explorations for generations to come. The feeling that things wonderful and unknown are yet to be discovered by future generations of astronomers and scientists is very exalting. The topics—such as the origins of the universe, the formation of Earth and of the eight other planets, the motion of the stars, and the extent of the space—are all subjects of wonderment for the human mind. However, modern technology has armed us with powers of observations and has given us the laws of science and the resourcefulness of creative minds so that we can further explore the mysteries of the universe with confidence, which was not possible for our ancestors. With these powers, we can explore the distant galaxies, follow the life cycles of the stars, and probe the distant reaches of the cosmos.

While exploring the outer universe, we come across heavenly bodies and objects that are very large in comparison with Earth and that are also at great distances from Earth. Some of the phenomena that we observe today have occurred a very long time ago, and we are still receiving the light from those occurrences. Since everything we see on Earth and in the outer space are an integral part of this vast and mysterious universe, it is to our advantage that we explore and know about it, at least superficially, without the mathematical and scientific details.

The next few sections will be devoted to various topics and phenomena of the universe explored by many scientists and astronomers who have spent their lifetimes to make knowledge of it available to us.

Thus, we owe it to ourselves to gain this knowledge and to pass it on to posterity. This is important because each new discovery gives rise to new knowledge of science with great new potential for practical uses impacting our lives. For example, who knew that the laws of physics discovered by Isaac Newton in the seventeenth century would have practical uses in the construction of modern-day machines, cars, airplanes, ships, buildings, bridges, and so on?

THE CELESTIAL SPHERE

Ancient astronomers believed that Earth is at the center of the universe. They also believed that all stars, including the Sun and the Moon, are attached to the inside surface of a huge hollow sphere that encircles Earth. This imaginary, hollow sphere called the celestial sphere is still used by modern-day astronomers as a useful tool for referencing the position of stars relative to Earth. There are a total of six thousand visible stars, and we can see about three thousand at one time above the horizon. There are another three thousand below the horizon on the other half of the celestial sphere. This is, in fact, only a small part of the universe visible to the naked eye.

The concept of the celestial sphere invented by the ancients is extremely useful today. By projecting Earth's equator out to the celestial sphere, we obtain the imaginary celestial equator, thus dividing the whole universe into northern and southern celestial hemispheres.

Figure 2-1 shows planet Earth at the center of the imaginary sphere called the celestial sphere.

This is very much similar to dividing Earth's surface into northern and southern hemispheres. Similarly, by projecting Earth's North Pole onto the celestial sphere, we obtain the imaginary north pole of the celestial sphere directly above the North Pole on Earth. In the same way, the south celestial pole is directly below the South Pole on Earth.

Using the celestial equator and celestial poles as the reference points, modern-day astronomers can exactly designate the position of any star or other heavenly body relative to the celestial equator in exactly the same way we can locate any city on Earth by its longitude and latitude relative to the equator. Thus, astronomers have mapped all the stars and other heavenly bodies in the same way geographers have mapped the whole Earth's surface and its geographical features.

The stars and other heavenly bodies are actually scattered in space at various distances from Earth in the range of ten to one thousand light-years away. These distances are so immense that all stars appear to be fixed to the celestial sphere and thus the name "fixed stars." Our Sun is the only star so close to Earth that it takes only eight and a half minutes for its light to reach us.

There is a fixed star at the north celestial pole called Polaris or pole star. This is a bright star used by navigators as a guide to locate their position while navigating in open seas when they cannot see any visible landmarks. Due to the inclination of Earth's axis of rotation, Polaris slowly traces out a circle among the northern stars.

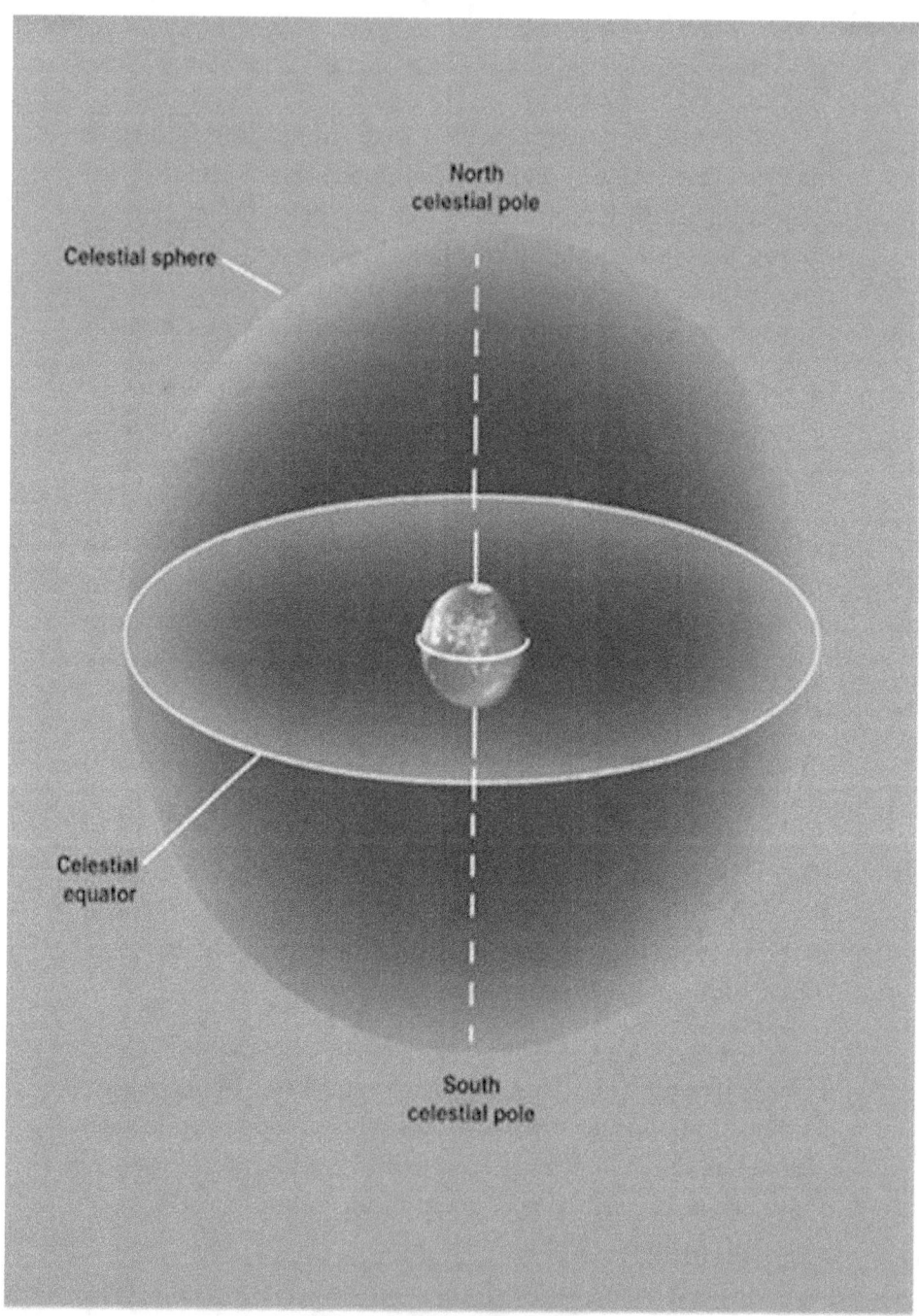

Fig. 2.1 Celestial Sphere

THE GALAXIES

Space, for the most part, is void and empty. At great intervals in this emptiness, there are flaring centers of heat and light called fixed stars, which are clustered and which move about in space in precise orbits. These clusters of stars are called galaxies. There are billions of stars in each galaxy, and there are billions of galaxies populating our universe. These galaxies have many shapes and sizes. Some are disk-shaped, like our own Milky Way galaxy, with arching arms; and some are ellipse-shaped. Most galaxies are grouped in clusters, stretching across the universe in huge fine patterns.

One of the first to inspire modern-day astronomers to explore the galaxies was the famous German philosopher Immanuel Kant, who, in 1755, had suggested that these faraway objects noted by ancients might be "island universes"—a vast collection of stars far beyond the limits of our Milky Way galaxy. Inspired by the suggestion of the German philosopher was an Irish nobleman named William Parsons, the Lord Duke of Rosse. William Parsons was very rich and very mechanical minded and had a fascination for machines as well as astronomy. Accordingly, he set about building a gigantic telescope to explore the farthest regions of the universe. In 1845, Parsons built a telescope sixty feet long and six feet in diameter. With this large telescope built in the nineteenth century, Lord Parsons examined many of the galaxies, which were cataloged by later astronomers. The famous galaxy discovered by Lord Parsons with his huge telescope is the spiral-shaped galaxy called the Whirlpool Galaxy so named because of its whirling appearance.

These advances in astronomy sparked interest of several young astronomers in discovering many more galaxies and their sizes and distances from Earth. Harlow

Shapley (1885–1972), a brilliant young American astronomer determined the size of our own Milky Way galaxy and became renowned for this discovery. In April 1920, a conference was held by the National Academy of Sciences in Washington, DC, and many questions on galaxies were discussed at this conference by two renowned American astronomers, Heber D. Curtis of California and Harlow Shapley. The Curtis-Shapley debate led to the question of the measurement of distance of the Whirlpool Galaxy from Earth. During this debate, no conclusive evidence could be put forward by Curtis or Shapley as to the distance of the Whirlpool Galaxy from Earth. This debate, however, sparked the interest of a brilliant young lawyer from Kentucky named Edwin Hubble enough to abandon his lucrative law practice in Kentucky and move to Chicago to study astronomy.

After completing his studies in Chicago, Hubble moved to California in 1923 to join Mount Wilson Observatory in Pasadena. Hubble's first great achievement was the measuring of the distance of the Whirlpool Galaxy from Earth. A rendering of the shape of this galaxy is shown in figure 2-2.

This first great achievement of Edwin Hubble, a lawyer turned astronomer, inspired him for further discoveries of many galaxies of several shapes and sizes. In the course of these discoveries, Hubble devised a system of classification for all his newly discovered galaxies. Hubble formulated this brilliant classification scheme and gave names to various galaxies. Some of these names include spirals, elliptical, barred spirals, giant elliptical, dwarf elliptical, and Magellanic. Magellanic galaxies are of irregular shapes not fitting into any of the regular shapes.

Fig. 2.2 Whirlpool Galaxy

Similarly, dwarf galaxies are much smaller than their giant counterparts with only a few million stars compared with the several billions in a giant galaxy.

With these achievements in exploring the outer reaches of the universe, Edwin Hubble proved himself to be a giant of an astronomer with an ambition and a purpose in life to do this pioneering work. There were no modern methods of space explorations and no modern technology of high-powered computers in the 1920s when Edwin Hubble was at the peak of his career. It was through sheer willpower, dogged determination, and diligence that Edwin Hubble achieved in life what he was destined to do.

Edwin Hubble presented his findings and discoveries to his peers at a meeting of the American Astronomical Society on December 30, 1924, and settled, once and for all, several questions of interest to all astronomers about the universe, the galaxies, and their distances from Earth. At this meeting, it was recognized by all brilliant minds that the universe is far larger and much more populated with many and much bigger galaxies than was previously thought by astronomers a generation earlier.

THE EARLY ASTRONOMERS

The present knowledge of the universe and heavenly bodies is rightly attributed to the work of inquiring minds of the Renaissance period that started in Italy around 1450 AD in the wealthy cities of Rome, Venice, Genoa, and Florence. The pioneering works of Copernicus, Kepler, Galileo, and Newton made the base for modern-day astronomers to further the knowledge we have today of the universe and the heavenly bodies. These people were brilliant, diligent, and well-read. They were very interested in the ancient works of Greek and Roman writers, philosophers, astronomers, and scientists. The foremost among the ancient classical was the Greek astronomer Ptolemy.

Very little is known about the personal life of Ptolemy, but he is regarded as a mathematical genius, an astronomer, and a great geographer of second century AD who lived in the city of Alexandria, Egypt, which was under the Greek rule at that time and established by Alexander the Great. Ptolemy wrote a book titled Almagest , which means "the greatest," where he described the heavenly bodies and their motions. At that time, there were only five known planets—Mercury, Venus, Earth, Saturn, and Jupiter. Earth was thought to be the center of the universe. It is well worth to point out that Ptolemy, the astronomer of 150 AD, is different from Ptolemy I of 300 BC, who was also Greek and a general of Alexander the Great. Ptolemy I became the ruler of Egypt after Alexander's empire split on his death. Ptolemy's model of the universe with only five planets and with Earth being the center was impressive indeed for second-century astronomers. Also, Ptolemy's model assumes that all heavenly bodies move in perfect circles. Though the model of Ptolemy was far from perfect, it was an inspiration to a Polish-born genius named Nicolaus Copernicus nearly one thousand three hundred years later.

Nicolaus Copernicus was born in 1473 to a wealthy Polish family. While studying medicine at the University of Krakow in Poland in the year 1491 (just a year before Christopher Columbus set off to his first voyage to America), Copernicus became very much interested in mathematics and astronomy. He later moved to Italy and studied law and mathematics and received a doctorate degree in law from the University of Ferrara in 1503. On graduating, Copernicus worked as a physician for his rich uncle. During this time, he devoted plenty of time to study astronomy and formulated his revolutionary ideas about Earth and its place in the universe. In the year 1510, he sent a summary of those ideas to some of his close friends and finally published them in 1543.

Copernicus's model of the universe has the Sun as the center and all known planets and Earth orbiting around it. However, later work of Kepler and Galileo further proved that Copernicus's model was only a convenient tool for more calculations by later astronomers the same way Ptolemy's model was just something of a base for Copernicus to start with one thousand three hundred years later. Thus, it is now accepted by all astronomers that all our ideas about how the universe works are simply models put forth to explain certain observations, calculations, and experimental results as best as we can. For the purpose of planning the rocket flight to the Moon, NASA uses Earth as the center of the model. But while calculating the flight of the space prop to planet Mars, NASA scientists treated the Sun in the model as being the center of the universe even though we know that the Sun itself orbits around the center of the Milky Way galaxy once in 250 million years. Thus, scientists use the simplest model they consider consistent with all the observations relative to a particular set of circumstances. They do not use the same model for all circumstances. A good practical example is the laws of Newtonian physics; they are perfect for all phenomena on the surface of Earth for the designing of machines, buildings, and bridges. For such models of engineering applications, we do not use Einstein's model of curved space and his laws of gravitation as applied to outer space in the cosmos.

MATTER AND ENERGY

Our universe, as we see and experience, is filled with an enormous amount of matter distributed sparsely in the vast emptiness of void space. Associated with the matter is also a vast amount of energy in the form of heat, light, electricity, magnetism, and electromagnetic waves of various types. Various types of electromagnetic waves are radio waves, microwaves, infrared rays, light waves, ultraviolet rays, x-rays, and gamma rays.

For discovering the mysteries of heavenly bodies—including the Sun, Moon, stars, and outer cosmos—scientists have devised high-powered telescopes and an optical device called spectroscope. It is now believed that all matters in the universe are basically made up of ninety-two known elements discovered so far on Earth. We know more about Mother Earth, being our life and blood, than we know about any other planet or star in the sky. Thus, having known all the elements of which Earth is made up, the spectroscope of light from any heavenly body is viewed against the background of comparison spectrum of known elements of Earth. By this comparison, it is estimated by what compositions and proportions the specific heavenly body is made up of.

In 1857, German-born chemist Robert Bunsen was the first scientist to invent a gas burner now called Bunsen burner, which produces a clean, colorless flame. When any chemical substance is sprinkled on the colorless flame of the burner, the flame produces a peculiar color specific to the elements of the substance. Bunsen's colleague Gustav Kirchhoff, another German-born physicist, suggested to Bunsen to study the light from the colored flame by passing it through a glass prism. By doing this, they discovered that spectrum from the colored flame showed a pattern of bright-colored lines against a black background. They next found, by using various substances and elements, that each element produces its own characteristic pattern of spectral lines. Thus, in 1859, they invented the technique of spectral analysis and spectroscopy used by scientists and astronomers alike to study the spectra of light from heavenly bodies. This technique is a very sure method to determine the chemical composition of far-off heavenly bodies. This is how an incidental discovery by Bunsen and Kirchhoff paved the way for astronomers to study the very far-off heavenly bodies and for scientists to discover more than a hundred elements of which Earth is made up.

Another example of incidental discovery is that of helium gas in the outer surface of the Sun in 1869 when astronomers were observing a solar eclipse. A new spectral line was discovered that was different from that of hydrogen of which bulk of the Sun is made up. Astronomers gave this new element the name helium (from Greek Helios meaning "sun"). Thirty years later, in 1895, helium was discovered on Earth as one of the gases emitted by a substance containing a compound of uranium.

Spectroscopy of the 103 elements of which Earth is made up will be discussed later in more detail. Here, it is sufficient to introduce this topic in connection with the exploration of heavenly bodies by astronomers. It is interesting to know that a technique used by astronomers to study far-off objects has immediate practical uses to study our own Mother Earth. This is very much analogous to the discovery made by Isaac Newton in the 1600s by observing the falling apple; the laws of gravitation and the motion of heavenly bodies so much useful in modern-day engineering and technology.

Out of the 103 elements of which all matter is composed, only a few were identified in the mid-1800s. Conclusively identified elements at that time were hydrogen, oxygen, carbon, iron, gold, and silver. The technique of spectral analysis invented by Bunsen and Kirchhoff led to fast discovery of more and more elements. Some of the rare elements—such as uranium, plutonium, and thorium—have been identified not long ago. In addition to the ninety-two naturally occurring elements, scientists have artificially produced eleven more elements in the laboratory by special techniques.

SUMMARY

Our universe is a wonderful act of creation that extends to infinity in all directions, filled with stars and many heavenly bodies at intervals. There are many identified galaxies in the universe. Our Milky Way galaxy is just one of them. Our Sun is one of the billions of stars in our Milky Way galaxy. The Sun is the source of all life on Earth. The universe is the eternal creation of God, who has infinite wisdom and power. Generations of astronomers and scientists have explored the universe. Polish-born Nicolaus Copernicus, Italian-born Galileo Galilei, German-born Johannes Kepler, and English-born Isaac Newton stand out among European astronomers. German-born chemist Robert Bunsen and his colleague physicist Gustav Kirchhoff, who is also German, invented the technique of spectroscopy to study the chemical composition of stars and other heavenly bodies. Irish-born Sir William Parsons discovered the famous Whirlpool Galaxy. Outstanding American astronomer Edwin Hubble measured the distance from Earth to the Whirlpool Galaxy and discovered many more galaxies. Harlow Shapley and Heber D. Curtis are among other outstanding American names in astronomy.

CHAPTER 3

OUR SOLAR SYSTEM

GENERAL

Our Sun, the Earth, and the eight other planets that have numerous moons, comets, and asteroids are all collectively called the solar system. Though commendable works of ancient astronomers like Copernicus, Kepler, Galileo, and Newton have shed much light on various heavenly bodies in our solar system, modern high-powered telescopes and space explorations have revealed a great deal more rich information about the heavens. Also, modern methods of spectroscopy and wavelength measurements are extremely helpful in gaining vast amounts of knowledge, which our ancestors did not have. For example, we precisely know the diameters of the Sun, Moon, Earth, and other planets and their mean distances from the Sun.

Knowing our position in the universe, knowing that our Sun is just one of the stars in our own galaxy, and knowing that there are many galaxies in our universe, we can now study very closely the phenomena that impact our daily lives on Earth. We make our living on our own planet, Earth; but almost daily, we see the Sun rising in the east and setting in the west with precise timing, accuracy, and reliability. Also, we experience the changes of seasons, variations of temperatures, and weather patterns, which are all related to our Earth's position relative to the Sun—the source of all life on Earth. We will dwell more on this subject in chapters 5, 6, and 7.

The names of the nine known planets orbiting the Sun in order of their distances from the Sun are Mercury, Venus, Earth, Mars, Jupiter, Saturn, Uranus, Neptune, and Pluto. Planet Earth has only one moon, some planets have more than one, and some have no moon at all. Since the Sun is at the center of the solar system and the cause of the gravitational pull that keeps all bodies in motion, we will start our discussion with this giant ball of fire so important to us.

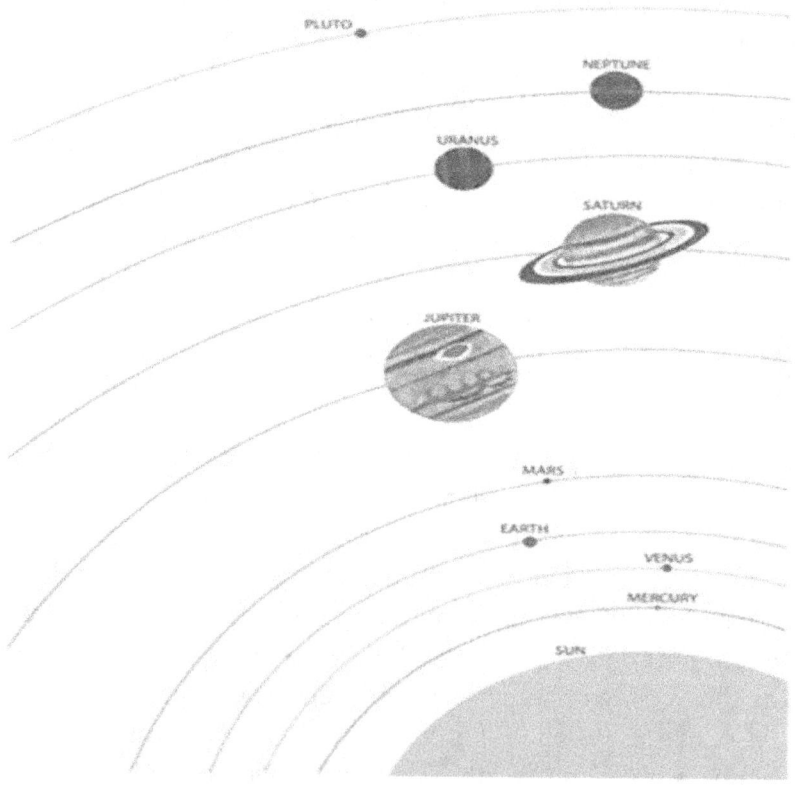

Fig. 3.1 Our Solar System

Fig. 3.2 Spectrum of Sunlight

THE SUN

Since Earth is our habitat and our home for millions of years, we know more about it than we know about any other planet. Similarly, since the Sun is our life giver, we know more about it than any other star in the heavens. Our knowledge about Earth and the Sun is of direct practical importance to our lives; whereas, the knowledge of the rest of the heavens is for our enlightenment and entertainment and for educational purposes only.

We begin our detailed exploration of our solar system by first taking a close look at the Sun. A most spectacular view of the Sun is at the time of its setting at the far end of a body of water when we see the big yellow ball above and its colorful reflection in the waves in the water below. We often ponder and wonder at this magnificent panorama. Many poets have been moved by the beauty of such scene whereas scientists have been inspired and moved to know about the giant ball of fire so far away from us and at the same time so close compared to the other stars. The Sun's closeness to us is not only of distance but also of relationship. If we do not see the Sun after several days of overcast skies, especially in the gloomy winter months, the spectacle of seeing the bright Sun and the uplifting feeling it brings is a joyful event. Similarly, after several hours of night-like darkness during which most human activities come to rest, rising up every morning to the tune of the rising Sun in the morning is an automatic joyful habit.

SIZE AND DISTANCE FROM EARTH

Though the Sun looks much bigger than other stars, in reality, it is one of the smaller stars. It looks bigger to us because it is closest to us. Its diameter is about 100 times the diameter of Earth (865,000 miles, to be exact). Its distance from Earth varies depending on the position of Earth in its orbit around the Sun. On average, it takes 8½ minutes for the Sun's light to reach us at a speed of 186,000 miles per second. Calculating this in terms of distance, it comes to about 93 million miles from Earth.

INTERIOR

The Sun is the only star in our Milky Way galaxy whose surface and interior details can be examined through Earth-based telescopes, and we do not need to resort to space probes. Although the Sun's interior is hidden from direct viewing through a telescope, scientists have used the laws of physics to calculate what is going on in the interior, such as its temperature, pressure, density, and thermonuclear reaction.

In the 1920s, British astronomer Arthur Eddington calculated that the temperature in the interior of the Sun is so high that at such a high temperature, four hydrogen (H) atoms can fuse together to form one helium (He) atom in accordance with this chemical equation: $4H \rightarrow He$.

In this nuclear reaction, a small amount of mass is lost with the release of a tremendous amount of heat energy according to Einstein's equation developed in 1905: $E = mc2$.

This process is called thermonuclear fusion and is going on in the Sun as it releases a tremendous amount of heat and other forms of energy, such as light, ultraviolet rays, gamma rays, and infrared rays. This thermonuclear reaction can occur only at very high temperature of several-million-degree Fahrenheit, which is estimated to be the temperature of the Sun's interior—approximately twenty-eight-million-degree Fahrenheit. Only a tiny fraction of heat energy given off by the Sun is usable on Earth. The rest is dissipated in outer space. The temperature on the surface is a lot less than in the interior. It is estimated to be ten-thousand-degree Fahrenheit.

Scientists have estimated the mass of the Sun to be 333,000 times the mass of Earth. It contains 92% hydrogen (H) and 8% helium (He). Thus, in the billions of years of the Sun's life, only 8% of the hydrogen is used up. Therefore, it can be assumed that the Sun is made to last till eternity, which is a very long time. That is all we need to know at this time and need not worry about its loss of mass.

Before we go to the discussion of other heavenly bodies in the Sun's family, some very interesting findings about the mysteries of the body of the Sun are worth noting. Just like geologists are able to study the Earth's interior structure using seismographs, astronomers are able to study the many characteristics of the Sun using the model of the Sun and the laws of physics. Some of these findings are summarized below.

1. The Sun is a stable star and is not undergoing any dramatic change. It is neither exploding nor collapsing nor significantly heating up or cooling off. It is thus in balance both thermally and mechanically.

2. The Sun has an atmosphere just like Earth's, but there is no sharp and hard boundary like the surface of Earth because all of the Sun's interior, outer layers, and atmosphere are gaseous.

3. By observing the position of sunspots from one day to the next, Galileo found that the Sun rotates about its axis once every four weeks.

4. The Sun has an interior core of one-half of the solar diameter where thermonuclear reaction

occurs. Heat energy from the core is transmitted by diffusion and then by convection to the Sun's surface.

5. Just like heat and light energy, there are several other types of waves emitted from its surface. One such form of energy is called the solar wind, which is a constant flow of charged particles (mostly electrons and protons) in all directions from the outermost surface of the Sun. As the charged particles of the solar wind approach Earth, the magnetic field of Earth repels and deflects them away, thus saving Earth from any damage. Similarly, Earth's ozone shield protects us from the Sun's dangerous radiation of ultraviolet rays. This is an assurance we have in the superb design of the Almighty Creator in protecting us from any danger.

Fig. 3.3 Our Moon

SUMMARY OF SUN'S DATA

Distance from Earth: 93 million miles

Diameter: $100 \times$ Earth's

Mass: 330,000 $\times$ Earth's

Average Density: 30 $\times$ Earth's

Chemical Composition: 92% hydrogen, 8% helium

Temperature: Surface: 10,000F°, Core: 28,000,000°F

Rotational Period: 28 days

Orbital Period about Center of Galaxy: 250 million years

Special Features: a source of gravitational force for all planets and a source of life on Earth

OUR MOON

We call it our Moon because it is literally ours as it orbits around our own planet. There are several other moons circling other planets in our solar system. In astronomical terms, Sun is a star, Earth is a planet, and Moon is a satellite. Our Moon is the closest companion to our Mother Earth as it is nearer to us than any other heavenly body and has been orbiting Earth precisely and faithfully once every twenty-eight days ever since the beginning of creation.

Our Moon is a large satellite with a diameter of about one-fourth the diameter of Earth and is at a distance of about a quarter million miles. A lot has been learned about the Moon ever since an American space program was started for reaching the Moon in the early 1960s after the Soviet sent an unmanned satellite Sputnik 1 around Earth in the fall of

1957. This was big news at the time and was the motivation behind America's ambitious space program to land on the Moon. The originators were the Wright brothers of Dayton, Ohio, who flew the first airplane in 1903. The Moon mission was accomplished in 1969 when the first American-manned spacecraft, Apollo 11, successfully landed on the Moon and was brought back successfully. It was a superb feat of American space technology unmatched in history. After this, there were five more manned lunar landings between 1969 and 1972. This experience in space technology gave rise to unmanned space probes to planets Mars, Venus, and the outermost planets by missions by Voyager 1 and Voyager 2.

These landings on the Moon and laboratory testing of samples of Moon rock revealed a lot of information previously unknown to astronomers. Though the size of the Moon and its distance had been calculated much earlier, but the knowledge of the Moon's surface features, chemistry of rocks, and the absence of water and air was not known before. The following are some of the important attributes of our Moon known to us.

1. Laboratory testing of Moon rock brought by astronauts revealed that there is no moisture in the samples. Moon is a bone-dry satellite incapable of supporting any life.

2. Moon rock cannot be called soil like the soil on Earth because our soil has the presence of decayed organic matter. Moon rock has no organic substance in it, which indicates that there has not been any plant or animal life on the Moon.

3. The Moon does not have any atmosphere like our Earth's atmosphere.

4. By viewing the Moon's surface features using high-powered telescopes or binoculars, we can observe that the

same side of the Moon always faces Earth. This proves that the Moon rotates about its own axis once every twenty-eight days—the same as its orbital period around Earth.

5. Though the Moon is thought to have an iron-rich core, it does not have any magnetic field like that of Earth as analyzed by seismographs left on the Moon by astronauts.

SUMMARY OF MOON'S DATA

Distance from Earth:	240,000 miles
Diameter:	2,160 miles
Rotational Period:	28 days
Orbital Period:	28 days
Chemical Composition:	Similar to Earth's with iron-rich core
Atmosphere:	None
Magnetic Field:	None

THE PLANET MERCURY

Starting with the planet Mercury, which is closest to the Sun, we will briefly discuss seven other distant planets before we will elaborate in great detail everything we know about planet Earth.

Mercury, though nearest, is still at an average distance of thirty-six million miles from the Sun and orbits around it once every eighty-eight days. It has a cratered surface, like the Moon, and has Earth-like interior with an iron-rich core and a magnetic field. Until 1974, we knew very little about this planet because of two reasons. First, it is very small; and second, it is so close to the Sun that it is difficult to see through Earth-based telescopes. We got our detailed knowledge about Mercury for the first time when space probe Mariner 10 coasted within 470 miles of the planet's surface. As the spacecraft closed in, scientists were amazed, looking at the moonlike pictures of Mercury with cratered surface. Having no water or atmosphere indicates that it is a barren, lifeless planet.

Daytime temperature at the equator of Mercury is measured to be 800°F, hot enough to melt lead and tin. Thus, Mercury is the hottest planet in our solar system. At midnight, the temperature of Mercury's equator dips to −280°F because of its loss of heat by radiation.

In size, Mercury is a little larger than our Moon (1⅓ times, to be exact) but much smaller than Earth—approximately one-third its size. The best time to see Mercury with the naked eye is when the planet is at the greatest distance from the Sun and appears as an evening star hovering low over the western horizon for a short time after sunset. This view of the planet lasts for a few days. Mercury can be seen as a morning star for a few days before sunrise over the eastern horizon. Though commonly called an evening star or a morning star, actually, it is not a star and does not have its own light but reflects the light of the Sun, just like our Moon does.

Mercury travels around the Sun faster than any other planet in our solar system. This is due to its closeness to the Sun, the greater force of gravitational pull of the Sun, and the greater angular speed in accordance with Newton's second law of motion. Naked-eye observations of Mercury are best made at dusk or at dawn, but best Earth-based telescopic views are obtained at midday when it is high above the horizon.

The discovery of large iron core of Mercury and its magnetic field was made by the magnetometers fitted in the spacecraft Mariner 10 when it hovered very close to the surface of Mercury in 1974. Though Mercury's magnetic field protects the planet from electrically charged dangerous solar wind, the absence of water and its atmosphere's extremes temperatures (800°F and −280°F) make life impossible. Thus, we are happy to have inhabited Earth where all conditions are favorable to life and its procreation. On close examination of other planets, we will find that our Earth is the best place known so far with abundance of life.

SUMMARY OF PLANET MERCURY'S DATA

Distance from Sun:	36 million miles
Diameter:	3,030 miles
Mass:	$1/20 \times$ Earth's
Average Density:	Same as Earth's
Surface Temperature:	Max.: 800°F, min.: −280°F
Chemical Composition:	70% iron, 30% other elements
Magnetic Field	$1/100 \times$ Earth's
Atmosphere:	Very little
Rotational Period:	59 days
Orbital Period:	88 days

Number of Moons: None

THE PLANET VENUS

Venus is the second planet from the Sun next to Mercury and is our immediate neighbor at a mean distance of twenty-six million miles from Earth. Planet Mars, the fourth from the Sun, is also our immediate neighbor on the other side away from the Sun and is at a distance of forty-nine million miles from us. Thus, we are sandwiched between Venus and Mars, our two neighboring planets in our solar system.

Like Mercury, Venus can be seen with the naked eye above the eastern horizon before sunrise and above the western horizon after sunset. Venus is very easy to identify because it is one of the brightest objects in the night sky next to the Moon. Earth-based telescopes' view of the planet shows a layer of thick clouds around it. During the 1960s, Russian spacecrafts have closed in on Venus and provided detailed pictures with a lot of information about this mysterious planet.

At first glance, Venus looks like Earth's twin planet. The two planets have almost the same diameter, same mass, same average density, and same surface gravity. Being closer to the Sun than Earth, Venus is exposed to more intense sunlight, which has transformed this earthlike planet into a chemically hostile one. During 1960s, while America was busy with landing astronauts on the Moon, Soviets focused on building a spacecraft that will land on Venus. This task was very frustrating to Soviet scientists because the spacecraft, after landing on the surface of Venus, would stop transmitting data to Earth. Finally, in 1970, a Soviet spacecraft succeeded to transmit data to Earth for a few seconds directly from the surface of the planet. This was big news at the time, similar to the American Moon landing in 1969. Though the Soviet spacecraft was unmanned, it was a success of unmatched proportions for sending a spacecraft to another planet forty-nine million miles away from Earth and transmitting data to Earth even for a few seconds.

Subsequent Soviet and American space probes that carried instruments landed on Venusian surface. The instruments aboard the spacecraft have detected high levels of sulfur dioxide and sulfuric acid in the upper atmosphere of Venus. Though Venus looks like Earth's twin, it is completely opposite in its atmospheric composition. Earth has abundant water in its oceans and atmosphere but very little carbon dioxide. In contrast, Venus's atmosphere contains much carbon dioxide but very little water. The atmosphere of Venus consists of 96% carbon dioxide, 4% nitrogen, and no oxygen. Other gases are sulfur dioxide, sulfuric acid clouds, and some moisture with compounds of sulfur.

It has been found that Venus does not have a Moon at all. Mercury and Venus are the only two planets in our solar system without any Moon. All other planets have one or more moons, which we will discuss later.

A few photographs of the surface of Venus taken by a Soviet spacecraft in 1981 show that the rocks on Venusian surface are orange colored. These may be due to the chemical action of sulfur dioxide and sulfuric acid. The best pictures of Venusian surface have come from the spacecraft Magellan that arrived on Venus in 1990 and orbited around the planet for five years. The pictures show that Venus is a desolate and barren planet without any signs of life and a lot of volcanic activity.

SUMMARY OF PLANET VENUS' DATA

Distance from the Sun: 67 million miles

Diameter: Same as Earth's

Mass: Same as Earth's

Average Density: Same as Earth's

Atmosphere: 96% carbon dioxide, 4% nitrogen

Tilt of Rotational Axis: 3.4°

Orbital Period: 226 days

Number of Moons: None

THE PLANET MARS

Mars is the fourth and last earthlike, terrestrial planet. It is at a distance of forty-nine million miles from Earth and orbits around the Sun once every two years. The other four planets—Jupiter, Saturn, Uranus, and Neptune—are called Jovian planets because of their large sizes and gaseous structures. The last and furthest planet, Pluto, does not fit into any category because of its very small size and special characteristics.

Before the 1976 landing of the unmanned American spacecraft Viking 1 on Mars, astronomers thought of the possibility of life on Mars. After viewing the pictures sent by Viking 1 and Viking 2 and studying the data from the spacecraft's instruments, it was found that Mars is as sterile and lifeless as our Moon. Direct chemical analysis of the Martian atmosphere by the Viking's instruments showed the atmosphere to be 95% carbon dioxide, 2.7% nitrogen, and 1.6% argon. The remaining are oxygen, carbon monoxide, and water vapor.

The lack of oxygen and water and the extremely low atmospheric pressure are the factors prohibiting life on Mars. Another factor is the extremely cold temperatures on the surface, which is measured to be −40°F by Viking instruments. The instruments showed that on the south pole region of Mars, the temperature drops so low that carbon dioxide freezes, causing the pressure to drop.

In most of the pictures received from Martian landings, the sky has a distinctively pinkish-orange color. This coloration is thought to be caused by fine-grained dust suspended in the Martian atmosphere. Although Martian atmosphere is very thin, its winds are sometimes very strong.

After the Viking landings on Mars's surface that lasted for a few weeks, their data showed that daily temperature variations are similar to Earth's but more pronounced. The daily temperature range on Mars is about three times greater than that on Earth because thin-dry Martian air does not retain heat as well as Earth's atmosphere does. The Viking landers' instruments also showed the absence of ozone layer. The Sun's dangerous ultraviolet radiation strikes Martian surface directly, making life impossible.

SUMMARY OF PLANET MARS'S DATA

Distance from Sun: 142 million miles

Diameter: ½ × Earth's

Mass: Same as Earth's

Average Density: ¾ × Earth's

Surface Temperature: −40°F

Rotational Period: 24½ hours

Orbital Period: 2 years

Number of Moons: 1

Atmosphere: 95% carbon dioxide, 2.7% nitrogen, 1.6% argon, 0.7% oxygen, carbon monoxide, and water vapor

Atmospheric Pressure: 1% of Earth's

Ozone Layer: None

CHAPTER 4

OUR SOLAR SYSTEM (CONTINUED)

THE PLANET JUPITER

Jupiter—the largest and heaviest planet of our solar system—is an active, vibrant, and multicolored world more massive than all other planets combined. Its mass is 320 times that of Earth and 2½ times the combined mass of all other planets, satellites, asteroids, meteoroids, and comets in our solar system. This is still a tiny fraction of the mass of the Sun, which is one thousand times the mass of Jupiter. Though these figures are very large, they can be easily comprehended—unlike the vastness of space—thanks to mathematics and the laws of physics, which give us the tools to calculate everything we know for sure.

Jupiter's average computed density is one-fourth of Earth's. This low average density is consistent with the structural composition of the planet. We know that Earth is a solid rock with a core of molten iron and nickel; whereas, Jupiter is predominantly light hydrogen and helium (82% hydrogen, 17% helium, and 1% combined small amounts of methane, ammonia, water vapor, and other gases) as determined by the instruments of spacecraft Voyager 1 in 1979 and Voyager 2 in the 1980s. Close-up views of the planet from the spacecraft show the remarkable colors of

Jupiter's clouds—red, orange, brown, yellow, and blue bands parallel to the planet's equator. These beautiful colors of Jupiter have been known to astronomers since the mid-1600s through Earth-based telescopes. Close-up pictures of the planet confirm the findings of astronomers 350 years earlier.

Jupiter has the fastest rate of rotation about its polar axis. It completes full rotation in less than ten hours, and its day is less than half-hour day. Radio waves transmitted from Jupiter indicate the presence of magnetic field around Jupiter just like Earth's magnetic field. Four American spacecraft flights passed Jupiter during the 1970s and revealed very interesting wind patterns in the planet's atmosphere, such as cyclones and anticyclones. Since Jupiter is mainly hydrogen and helium in solid, liquid, and gaseous states, the gaseous hydrogen and helium make Jupiter's atmosphere very turbulent. Earth-based telescopic data and Voyager data show that wind speeds in Jupiter's atmosphere are remarkably stable even though the colorful bands change quite rapidly.

The internal structure of the planet, as determined by spacecraft's instruments, is solid, rocky hydrogen and helium. Above the solid core is the mantle of liquid hydrogen capped by gaseous hydrogen.

Because of Jupiter's rapid rotation, the liquid hydrogen generates a powerful magnetic field around it in much the same way as Earth's magnetic field. Jupiter's magnetic field is nineteen thousand times more powerful than that of Earth's because of Jupiter's great mass and is slightly inclined from the planet's axis of rotation. Strangely, the orientation of Jupiter's magnetic field is the reverse of Earth's magnetic field. In other words, magnetic compass needle on Jupiter will point toward the south pole as against toward north on Earth. This reversion of orientation is due to the reverse direction of motion of liquid hydrogen in Jupiter's mantle as opposed to the direction of motion of molten iron and nickel in Earth's core. These are very interesting things to know about the planets in our solar system even though we are not directly affected by these the same way we are affected by the powers of the Sun.

SUMMARY OF PLANET JUPITER'S DATA

Distance from Sun:	482 million miles
Diameter:	$10 \times$ Earth's
Mass:	$320 \times$ Earth's
Average Density:	$\frac{1}{4} \times$ Earth's
Chemical Composition:	82% hydrogen, 17% helium, 1% methane, ammonia, water, and other gases
Magnetic Field:	$19,000 \times$ Earth's
Rotational Period:	10 hours
Orbital Period:	12 years
Number of Moons:	15
Special Features:	Turbulent winds and colorful bands patterns parallel to its equator

THE PLANET SATURN

Saturn is another spectacular and colorful planet orbiting our Sun at a distance of 885 million miles from the center of the Sun and completes one orbit around it in a little less than thirty years. Planet Saturn is as large as Jupiter in size but has only one-third the mass of Jupiter. Why is there so big a difference in masses while diameters are about equal? Perhaps it's due to density and gravity compression in Jupiter. Average density of Jupiter is one-fourth that of Earth while Saturn's is one-eighth of Earth's.

The magnificent and colorful rings of Saturn make this a unique planet in our solar system. Saturn is so far away from us that Earth-based telescopes can give us only the view of its largest features. Very fine details were viewed only from the pictures sent back by Voyager 1 in the early 1980s. Astronomers have known for more than a century that Saturn's rings are not of solid, rigid matter but are made up of an indefinite number of unconnected particles that each circle around Saturn in its own orbit. In 1857, a Scottish astrophysicist named James Clark Maxwell was the first scientist to prove mathematically that the rings are not rigid sheets of matter but are composed of the tiny moons of Saturn. The rings are so bright that the particles that form the rings must be highly reflective of sunlight. Astronomers have long suspected the rings to be made of ice and ice-coated rock, but only in the 1970s was it confirmed when the spectrum of the rings showed infrared lines of that of frozen water. Additional measurements from instruments of the Voyager spacecraft in the early 1980s showed that the temperature of the rings varied between −290°F in sunshine and −330°F in Saturn's shadow. These temperatures are so low that water remains permanently frozen that give the rings colorful brightness.

Fig. 4.1 Planet Saturn

Saturn's rings are in the planet's equatorial plane, which is tilted at 27° from the plane of Saturn's orbit. Because of this tilt, Earth-based telescopic view of the planet shows the rings at various angles depending on the planet's position relative to the Sun in its orbit. NASA scientists measured the brightness of the rings from many angles as the spacecraft flew past the planet and also calculated the sizes of particles that make the rings from the data transmitted by Voyager's instruments.

The variation of colors of Saturn's rings from one ring to the next give important clues about the composition of the particles of the rings. The color differences exaggerated by computer processing indicated that main chemical constituent is frozen water with traces of other chemicals coating the surfaces of the ice particles. These other chemicals could not be identified by space scientists, but ice is definitely the bulk of the matter.

Astronomers have known for centuries Saturn's six moons, but it was only after Voyager 1 spacecraft's flyby that the discovery of several other moons was possible. Now it is known that Saturn has at least fifteen moderate-sized moons ranging from 80 miles to 250 miles diameter. Voyager cameras also discovered two tiny satellites that follow orbits around Saturn—one on either side of the F ring. Gravitational forces of two satellites keep the F ring particles in place.

Spectroscopic observations show that Saturn's atmosphere is made up of methane, ammonia, and water vapor. These compounds are the simplest combinations of nitrogen, carbon, oxygen, and hydrogen. Also, wind speeds near Saturn's equator are found to reach one thousand miles per hour. Voyager spacecraft also revealed that Saturn is composed of 88% hydrogen, 11% helium, and 1% of all other elements combined—very much similar to Jupiter's. Saturn's internal structure is also very much like Jupiter's with an interior core of solid hydrogen surrounded by a mantle of liquid hydrogen capped by gaseous hydrogen.

Rotational period of Saturn is a little over ten hours. Due to the rapid speed and large diameter, Saturn has a strong magnetic field. Because of cold temperatures, lack of free oxygen, plenty of ammonia and methane, there is no chance of life on this far-off, cold planet.

It is interesting to note the differences between the Sun's hydrogen and helium versus Saturn's and Jupiter's hydrogen and helium. The Sun is a star and a source of heat and light energy that emanate from its core by thermonuclear conversion of hydrogen to helium at temperatures of millions of degrees Fahrenheit while hydrogen and helium in the core of Jupiter and Saturn are frozen solid at extremely low temperatures. This is a miraculous phenomenon outside the scope of any theory or reasoning but only subject to the will of the Creator.

SUMMARY OF PLANET SATURN'S DATA

Distance from Sun: 885 million miles

Diameter: $10 \times$ Earth's

Mass: $100 \times$ Earth's

Average Density: $\frac{1}{8} \times$ Earth's

Chemical Composition: 88% hydrogen, 11% helium, 1% all other elements

Temperature: $-290°F$ to $-330°F$

Magnetic Field: Strong

Atmosphere: Methane, ammonia, and water vapor

Tilt of Equator: $27°$

Rotational Period: 10 hours

Orbital Period: 29 years

Number of Moons: 15

Special Features: Colorful rings around its equator

THE PLANET URANUS

Next to Saturn, but much smaller in size is the planet Uranus—the twin of Neptune in size, shape, and chemical composition. Through powerful Earth-based telescopes, Uranus appears as a small greenish-blue disk. This planet looks so small because it is very far away from us—about twenty times farther than we are from the Sun.

Very little was known about planet Uranus until Voyager 2 spacecraft, after nearly eight and a half years of coasting through interplanetary space, finally reached Uranus in January of 1986. During the few days that pictures and data poured in, we learned more about this remote world than we had learned in the two centuries when Uranus was first discovered. This is indeed a remarkable feat of American aviation technology, pioneered only a century ago by the Wright brothers, Wilbur and Orville of Dayton, Ohio, when they succeeded in flying the first wooden airplane in 1903.

It was already known from observations through Earth-based telescopes that the axis and rotation of Uranus lies very closely in the plane of its orbit. Consequently, as the planet moves around the Sun in its orbit, Uranus's north and south poles alternately point toward or away from the Sun, producing long seasons. Since the orbital period of Uranus around the Sun is equal to eighty-four Earth years, each season of Uranus—its spring, summer, fall, and winter—is each equal to twenty-one years, a very long time indeed. Though the rotation period of Uranus is only sixteen hours long—eight hours daylight and eight hours nighttime—and is not too different from ours on Earth, long seasons of twenty years each are very peculiar. If we were living on Uranus, we might get accustomed to it, but it would be very boring indeed. Again, this is the only peculiar planet with its axis flat in the plane of its orbit as if it is rolling on its belly.

By the time Voyager 2 approached Uranus, the planet's north pole was directly aimed at the Sun, and very clear, illuminated pictures of Uranus's northern hemisphere were transmitted by cameras of Voyager 2. No clouds or any other atmospheric features were seen by the cameras except some smog-like haze over the north pole.

The instruments of Voyager 2 revealed that Uranus has a strong magnetic field that is fifty times stronger than Earth's magnetic field. The magnetic axis of the planet is tilted 60° from the axis of rotation. This inclination is peculiar because planets that have magnetic fields have invariably the magnetic axes nearly aligned with their rotational axes. Voyager 2 also discovered that Uranus has many moons that revolve around the planet in its equatorial plane and also a system of thin, dark rings. Voyager 2 discovered ten additional moons of Uranus, thus making a total of fifteen with the five known earlier.

Voyager 2 instruments indicate that the internal structure of Uranus has rocky core, and the outer layers are predominantly composed of hydrogen and helium in gaseous state. Also, the temperature of the upper layers is measured to be as low as −351°F, which is the freezing point of methane gas. This gas absorbs red light, thus giving Uranus a blue-green color in the Voyager 2 photographs.

SUMMARY OF PLANET URANUS'S DATA

Distance from Sun:	1,780 million miles
Diameter:	4 × Earth's diameter
Mass:	15 × Earth's mass
Average Density:	¼ × Earth's density
Chemical Composition:	Hydrogen and helium
Temperature:	−351°F
Magnetic Field:	Strength, 50 × Earth's
Tilt of Rotational Axis:	60°
Rotational Period:	16 hours
Orbital Period:	84 years
Number of Moons:	15
Special Features:	Only planet lying flat and rolling on its belly

THE PLANET NEPTUNE

In size, Neptune is of about the same diameter as Uranus. Because of Neptune's great distance from Earth (2,790 million miles), it is also seen as a tiny, hazy disk with a greenish-blue tinge similar to planet Uranus when viewed through powerful Earth-based telescopes. However, the arrival of American spacecraft Voyager 2 at Neptune in August 1989 was the highlight of one of NASA's most ambitious and successful missions of interplanetary space probes. After seeing Neptune as a small blue disk by generations of astronomers through Earth-based telescopes, NASA scientists were jubilant at the close-up pictures and the wealth of data sent back by Voyager 2 instruments.

Neptune is found so cold that its atmospheric temperature is measured to vary between −350°F at the equator and poles to about −300°F at midlatitudes. The atmosphere of Neptune is primarily composed of hydrogen and helium with an admixture of methane. The presence of methane is detected from the spectroscopic analysis. Methane absorbs visible wavelengths of infrared rays of red and yellow colors but not blue and green colors of shorter wavelengths. Thus, sunlight reflected from Neptune's atmosphere is depleted of reds and yellows, making the planet appear greenish-blue.

Neptune is found to have a strong magnetic field. Neptune's magnetic field is found to be inclined 47° to its axis of rotation and oriented opposite to that of Earth's. This is also the case with the three other Jovian planets—Jupiter, Saturn, and Uranus. From the periodic emissions of radio signals, Neptune's period of rotation is calculated to be sixteen hours. Also, its orbital period is known to be 165 years by observations from Earth-based telescopes.

SUMMARY OF PLANET NEPTUNE'S DATA

Distance from Sun: 2,790 million miles

Diameter: 4 × Earth's diameter

Mass: 15 × Earth's mass

Average Density: ¼ × Earth's density

Chemical Composition: Hydrogen, helium, methane

Temperature: Max.:	−300°F, min.: −350°F
Magnetic Field:	50 × Earth's field
Rotational Period:	16 hours
Orbital Period:	165 years
Number of Moons:	1
Special Features:	Neptune is surrounded by a system of dark rings.

THE PLANET PLUTO

The farthest and smallest planet of our solar system was discovered by Clyde W. Tombaugh in the year 1930 as a faint, starlike object in the sky that shifts its position from night to night. A peculiarity of this lately discovered ninth planet in our solar system is that its only moon, Charon, which was discovered in the year 1978, is half the size of Pluto and orbits around it in the same direction as the spinning direction of Pluto. Furthermore, Charon's orbital period of six and a half days around Pluto is the same as the spinning period of Pluto. Therefore, Pluto always keeps the same side facing Charon. If we were living on Pluto facing Charon, we would see Charon as a stationary object that is always in one position as if it were hanging from the sky. If we were on the other side of Pluto that is not facing Charon, we would never see Charon at all.

The average densities of Pluto and its satellite Charon are found to be equal. These densities are computed from the data recorded by the instruments aboard the spacecraft Voyager 2, which is now headed out of our solar system after eight and a half years of interplanetary missions.

For many years to come, Voyager 2 will continue probing the outer cosmos, and its instruments will record the electrical pulses of solar wind at extreme distances from the Sun and may reach the influence boundaries of another sun and another solar system. Who knows? At present, NASA scientists have no plans of changing the direction of Voyager 2 to return to Earth.

Similar to the Moon landing of 1969, this mission of Voyager 2 is another highlight of the American space exploration program and will remain a landmark in the history of aviation.

SUMMARY OF PLANET PLUTO'S DATA

Distance from the Sun 3,600 million miles

Diameter	1,430 miles
Mass	1/500 of Earth's mass
Average Density	⅓ of Earth's density
Rotational Period	6½ days
Orbital Period	248 years
Number of Moons	1

ASTEROIDS, COMETS AND METEOROIDS

ASTEROIDS

In addition to nine planets there are many smaller heavenly objects orbiting the Sun in fixed orbits between the orbits of Mars and Jupiter. In the late 1700s, a young German astronomer named Johann Elert Bode predicted through his calculations that there was an undiscovered planet between Mars and Jupiter. With Bode's prediction, astronomers started looking for this missing planet, which led to the discovery of the asteroid belt.

The first ever asteroid discovered was by a Sicilian Italian astronomer named Giuseppe Piazzi in 1801. On January 1, the day of the start of the nineteenth century, Piazzi noticed in his telescope a dim star that shifted its position slightly over the next several nights. Piazzi thought this was the missing planet and named it Ceres after the patron goddess of Sicily. Later, other astronomers observed Ceres and discovered that it had a diameter of about six hundred miles and cannot be called a planet.

In 1802, a German astronomer Heinrich Olbers discovered another dim starlike object that moved against the background of fixed stars and named it Pallas after the Greek goddess of wisdom. Like Ceres, Pallas was also found to be very small with a diameter of about half of that of Ceres. Therefore, Pallas was not considered the missing planet either. At this point, astronomers called these two objects asteroids.

After the discovery of asteroids Ceres and Pallas, astronomers started looking with keen interest for more of these small bodies that orbit the Sun between Mars and Jupiter. Consequently, in 1891, German astronomer Max Wolf invented a very clever technique for the discovery of numerous more asteroids in the asteroid belt. The technique is called astrophotography. With this new technique, astronomers could aim a camera-equipped telescope at the stars and take long exposures. If an asteroid happened to be in the field of view of the telescope, it would leave a long trail on the photographic plate because of the asteroid's motion relative to the fixed stars. Using this technique, Wolf discovered 228 new asteroids.

Techniques developed by Max Wolf became so popular with astronomers that over a period of one hundred years, astronomers discovered twenty-nine thousand asteroids orbiting the Sun between Mars and Jupiter. Out of twenty-nine thousand asteroids, only nine thousand have been defined to have well-known orbits. The orbits of the rest of them have never been determined. The orbits of all officially discovered asteroids are published annually in the Soviet Catalogue of Minor Planets with the discoverer astronomer's name.

COMETS

Comets are the most spectacular and fiery heavenly body that orbit the Sun at great distances in elliptical orbits. A comet has a well-defined head and a long tail. Most comets seem to come close to Earth only once, but others seem to visit us on a definite schedule. Halley's comet—named after Edmund Halley (1656–1742), a British astronomer who observed it first in 1682—is the most famous one. Edmund Halley calculated the orbital period of this comet to be seventy-six years. The comet was visible from Earth in 1910 and then again in 1986.

Comets are made up of chunks of rock and dusty chunks of ice. When a comet passes near the Sun, solar heat of radiation vaporizes the comet's ice and produces a long, flowing tail. After many such passes near the Sun, all the comet's ice is depleted, leaving only the dust and the chunks of rock. These chunks of rock then fall on Earth in the form of a meteor shower. Thus, meteoroids and asteroids are much alike as both are big chunks of rock. When the object is more than a few hundred miles in diameter, it is called an asteroid. Smaller objects are called meteoroids.

SUMMARY OF OUR SOLAR SYSTEM

Before we start a detailed discussion of planet Earth, it is appropriate here to have an overview of what we have learned about the other eight planets.

We have learned that the nearest planet, Mercury, and the farthest planet, Pluto, are much smaller in size than Earth. Venus and Mars are about the same size as Earth; whereas, Jupiter and Saturn are ten times bigger, and Uranus and Neptune approximately four times Earth's size. Also, there was a pattern found—that is, the nearer a planet is to the Sun, the shorter the orbital period is. Mercury's orbital period is 88 days; Venus's, 226 days; and Earth's, 365¼ days. As the planet's distance from the Sun gets bigger, the orbital period gets bigger as well. Mars's distance from the Sun is 1½ times that of Earth's, and its orbital period is about 2 times of Earth's. Jupiter's distance is 5 times that of Earth's, and its orbital period is about 12 times. Saturn's distance is 10 times that of Earth's; its orbital period is times; and so on. Finally, Pluto's distance from the Sun is 40 times that of Earth's, and its orbital period is 248 times that of Earth's. Also, it has been found that the orbits of all the planets are approximately in the same plane as Earth's orbit.

In conclusion, we can say that the foregoing discussion of the eight planets is ample to satisfy our curiosity, is of great value as intellectual enrichment, and is an entertaining read. Moreover, the discussion throws light on the history of the endeavors of our long-gone ancestors, scientists, astronomers, and mathematicians in solving the mysteries of creation. Also summarized are the contributions of most recent generations of scientists, which include the famous names of Copernicus (1473–1543), Kepler (1571–1630), Galileo (1564–1642), Newton (1642–1727), and Einstein (1870–1955). Furthermore, our knowledge of far-off planets millions of miles away from Earth is a tribute to our space-age heroes—Americans and Soviets whose dedicated contributions made this knowledge possible. The inspiring stories of dedication and courage of the Wright brothers of Dayton, Ohio, in 1903; the first space satellite Sputnik 1 by the Soviets in 1957; the American Moon landing of 1969; and the latest NASA missions of Voyager 2 are all the wonders of the mind of our own species, Humania, as distinct from over a million species inhabiting our planet.

From the foregoing discussion, we have learned that Earth is not only the best place to live but also the only place God has created for us to make our living in accordance with His plans and His scheme of things. Planets Mercury and Venus, being too close to the Sun, are too hot; and the rest of the six planets—Mars, Jupiter, Saturn, Uranus, Neptune, and Pluto—are too cold, barren, and devoid of oxygen and water, which are necessary for life. There may or may not be any other planet in the galaxies where there could be an abundance of life similar to Earth's; we do not know. All we know for sure on learning from Voyager 2 spacecraft is that our Mother Earth is the only planet in our solar system capable of supporting life and all our needs. This is our inheritance for taking care of her very responsibly as she takes care of us exceedingly well.

CHAPTER 5

OUR PLANET EARTH

THE BEGINNING

"In the beginning God created the heavens and the earth. The earth was formless and void, and darkness was over the surface of the deep; and the Spirit of God was moving over the surface of the waters." NAS Bible

The beauty of our blue-and-white planet was first observed in 1968 by astronauts on board the spacecraft Apollo 8 on their way to the Moon. This was to be the first of many history-making events of NASA's ambitious space exploration program that started in the late 1950s. Apollo astronauts described the beauty of planet Earth as most invitingly spectacular. The pictures taken by Apollo 8 cameras transmitted to NASA space centers were the first of its kind of the view of the colorful globe from a far-off distance in space.

THEORIES AND HYPOTHESES

Modern scientists, geologists, astronomers, and mathematicians focus their attention and knowledge to estimate the life of our planet Earth, which is still a mystery. However, some of the hypotheses put forth in the last two hundred years are worth noting.

Fig. 5.1 Our Planet Earth

PIERRE-SIMON, MARQUIS DE LAPLACE'S HYPOTHESIS

In the 1800s, French mathematician Simon de Laplace put forth his hypothesis that a mass of hot gas in space suddenly started spinning faster and faster. A portion of this mass became the Sun, and the torn-away portions cooled and became planets. Laplace, in his hypothesis, had all the planets spinning in the same direction. Later astronomers investigated and found that planet Uranus spins in a direction opposite to that of all other planets. This reversed spinning of Uranus could not be explained by Laplace's hypothesis, and thus, the hypothesis was rejected.

CHAMBERLIN-MOULTON HYPOTHESIS

American scientists T. C. Chamberlin and F. R. Moulton, both professors at the University of Chicago, advanced a hypothesis in the early 1900s. According to this hypothesis, another huge star similar to our Sun passed by the Sun and caused gravitational tidal bulges on its surface. These gaseous bulges whirled around the Sun by its gravitational forces and eventually formed nine planets, including our Earth. Later scientists rejected this hypothesis on the grounds that these gases torn away from the Sun would have continued exploding by thermonuclear reaction and would have no time to cool.

GERARD KUIPER'S HYPOTHESIS

Dutch American astronomer Gerard P. Kuiper advanced still another hypothesis that when the Sun was formed from a mass of hot gases, the outer masses ringed the Sun and kept condensing and cooling and became planets.

FRED HOYLE'S HYPOTHESIS

English astronomer Fred Hoyle offered his own hypothesis that the Sun, at one time, had a companion star. This companion star exploded, and the erupting gases condensed and formed Earth and eight other planets.

THE BIG BANG THEORY

In 1946, some astronomers put together yet another new concept known as the big bang theory. According to this theory, the whole matter of the universe was just a single mass fifteen billion years ago. This mass exploded for some reason or another, and the gases from that explosion produced stars and our Sun. Some stars exploded to form other stars and planets. The masses that cooled became planets, and those that contained thermonuclear reactions became stars like our Sun.

Whatever the beginnings of planet Earth are, scientists agree that our planet has been in existence for a very long time. In the early days, it spun and whirled in its orbit around the Sun as a fiery hot mass that slowly cooled; and the top cooled surface formed the crust. On average, the crust is eight to ten miles thick. Under the crust is a hot mantle 1,800 miles thick, and below the mantle is a core 4,400 miles in diameter. The core contains molten iron and nickel continuously in motion, creating Earth's magnetic field. The temperatures at the core are extremely high— about 10,000°F.

EARTH'S GRAVITATION

Gravity is the force with which any two masses attract each other. Isaac Newton was the first scientist for the famous discovery of the law of gravitation named after him. The falling apple is a very well-known story that set young Newton's imagination into motion, which made him the greatest scientist of the seventeenth century. Since Earth has a big mass, it attracts all other objects that have masses. The force of attraction is proportional to the product of two masses and is inversely proportional to the square of the distance between the centers of the masses. This is called Newton's law of gravitation. By several experiments,

Newton determined the constant of gravitation G. Newton further explored the laws of motion of heavenly bodies—such as the Moon, Earth, and other planets—based on the law of gravitation. He then discovered that all heavenly bodies move because of the forces of gravitation. The Sun possesses a big mass and, by its forces of gravitation, makes Earth and all planets orbit around it. What causes gravity? This is the law of the Almighty Creator of the universe, and no scientist can question it or hypothesize about it.

Due to gravitational forces of the Sun, Earth moves around it in an elliptical orbit. For hundreds of years, astronomers believed that Earth was the center of the universe and also of the solar system. Polish astronomer Nicolaus Copernicus (1473–1543) proposed that the Sun and not Earth was at the center of the solar system. Similarly, for hundreds of years before Christopher Columbus, people believed that Earth was flat; but Columbus, by his brave voyages, changed that thinking.

A German astronomer named Johannes Kepler worked out the three laws of motion of Earth and the other planets. The laws are called Kepler's laws of motion of planets, which is similar to Newton's laws of motion.

KEPLER'S FIRST LAW

The orbit of Earth and all other planets around the Sun is an ellipse with the Sun located at the middle of two foci of the ellipse. Because two foci of the eclipse are so close, the orbit is very nearly a circle.

KEPLER'S SECOND LAW

A planet does not move about the Sun at a constant speed throughout its orbit. The speed is slowest when the planet is farthest from the Sun and fastest when closest to it.

KEPLER'S THIRD LAW

This law states that the orbital period of a planet depends on the planet's average distance from the Sun. The farther a planet is from the Sun, the longer its orbital period. Thus, the orbital periods of Mercury and Venus are shorter than Earth's orbital period, which is 365¼ days; and the orbital periods of Mars and all other planets are much longer than 365¼ days.

MATERIAL RESOURCES OF EARTH

In scientific terminology, matter is a term that has a meaning very much different from the commonly used term in general conversation. The term matter of fact or what's the matter has meanings different from scientific meanings. In science, matter means "a substance that possesses mass or weight" as distinguished from energy. Thus, our planet Earth is made up of matter of huge mass. Here, again, we are talking about nonliving matter, like soil and rock. Through scientific research, new knowledge of the matter or materials existing on Earth is obtained; and new ways of using these resources are developed.

Scientists learn from the experiments and ideas of other scientists; and each build on the genius of those who came before. Very often, a new discovery or invention results after long periods of time with the combined efforts of many scientists from several countries of the world.

Our planet Earth has inexhaustible material resources for us to make use of wisely. By applying the knowledge of material resources, man continues to improve his life, like the use of wood in houses, steel in buildings, concrete in bridges, aluminum in airplanes, copper in electrical appliances, synthetic fabric in clothes, and so on. In fact, everything is used wisely and economically.

All matter is made up of certain basic substances called elements. An element is "a substance that cannot be split into any simpler form by ordinary means." For example, iron, aluminum, carbon, oxygen, hydrogen, silver, and copper are elements. Two or more elements may be combined to form a new substance called a compound. Thus, water is a compound of two elements: oxygen and hydrogen. This is just one of the miracles of science—oxygen gas combines with another hydrogen gas to form water. Likewise, water can be decomposed into oxygen and hydrogen by using electric current in a process called hydrolysis. In their natural states, atmospheric oxygen and hydrogen do not combine to form water nor does water decompose into oxygen and hydrogen.

Presently, there are ninety-two known naturally occurring elements on Earth. These elements form the chemical composition of all matters in planets, the Sun, and the stars. The names of all elements are represented by various symbols, such as Al for aluminum, C for carbon, H for hydrogen, O for oxygen, and so on. When a compound is made up of two or more elements, scientific representation of elements in that compound is denoted by a chemical formula, such as H_2O for water, CO_2 for carbon dioxide, and NaCl for sodium chloride. In addition to ninety-two elements, there are eleven artificial laboratory-made radioactive elements, making a total of 103 elements in the periodic table developed by Henry Moseley (1877–1915), an English scientist. Originally, Russian scientist Dmitri Mendeleev also developed a table of elements known as Mendeleev's Table. Uranium is the heaviest naturally occurring element, and hydrogen is the lightest. Moseley's Table, on the other hand, is based on the atomic number of the element, which is the number of protons in the nucleus of the atom of the element. No two elements have the same atomic number. In any stable atom of an element, the number of protons in the nucleus is equal to the number of electrons orbiting around the nucleus.

All nonliving matter and living beings are made up of compounds of the basic elements in varying proportions. It is fascinating to study the interaction of elements in plants and animals and the complex subjects of chemistry and biology.

All matter is classified into three different states: solids, liquids, and gases. Most matter occurs in its natural state. However, some matter can occur in all three states at different temperatures as is water a liquid at normal temperature, solid when frozen, and steam when boiled.

FORMS OF ENERGY

Energy is a scientific term that has a specific meaning for the specific form of energy. The term is widely used in everyday language, such as the energy level being high or low when referring to physical fitness. In scientific terms, energy means one of the following:

- heat energy

- light energy

- electrical energy

- nuclear energy

Scientists and engineers are working and researching constantly for new knowledge on how to use material resources the best possible way to develop energy sources of Earth. Here, we will briefly discuss the forms of energy, the conversion of one form into the other, and the beneficial use of each form.

HEAT ENERGY

This is the form of energy possessed by a body that has mass and high temperature. Temperature is a measurement of the degree of warmth or coldness of the object. Heat energy travels from a body with high temperature to another adjacent body with a lower temperature. There are three modes of transfer of heat energy. These are conduction, convection, and radiation. Conduction occurs when heat travels from one solid to another solid. When we put a thermometer in the mouth to check our temperature, the heat flow from under the tongue to the thermometer is called conduction. The heat transfer known as convection occurs in liquids and gases. Finally, radiation is the travel of heat energy by wave action similar to the travel of light. The heat from the Sun coming to Earth is by radiation traveling through empty space with a distance of ninety-three million miles in the short time of eight and a half minutes. This is again one of the wonders of the science of creation.

Whether Earth is of solar origin or is independently created, we know that below the eight-mile-thick crust is a very hot and plastic mantle that is 1800 miles thick. These findings are made by modern methods of seismology. Also, it is found that the temperature of the crust increases by several degrees with every depth of a few hundred feet. This is found in deep coal mines and also in oil-well drilling. Thus, with the very hot core and mantle, Earth has its own stable, inexhaustible heat energy. It is also known that the average temperature of soil at ten feet below the surface remains constant throughout the year, thus conserving the heat energy of Earth.

LIGHT ENERGY

Like heat, light is also a very useful form of energy that comes from the Sun—the source of all life on Earth. Without sunlight, no plant can grow; and we would not have food on our table without the growth of plants and vegetables.

In addition to food, light is a blessing in another way. Without light, there would be darkness everywhere; and we would not be able to see anything. Our eyes become useless without light. You can experience this in a completely dark room full of furniture and other things. Eyes cannot see anything. Both light energy and our eyes are a great blessing to us for us to see the world around us.

Our eyes contain nerve endings that are sensitized by light energy. When light stimulates our eyes' nerve endings, nerve impulses travel along the optic nerve from the eye to the brain, which records the picture of the object in the brain.

The theories on light and the study of optics is a whole branch of science and a specialty in itself. Isaac Newton was one of the leading scientists in the seventeenth century to give us a great deal of knowledge about light energy and optics in addition to his laws of gravitation and the laws of motion of bodies.

ELECTRICAL ENERGY

Many scientists in the seventeenth century, including Isaac Newton, noted similarities between the lightning in the skies and the static electric spark produced by rubbing a glass rod on silk cloth. But no one did any experimentation until Benjamin Franklin—American politician, philosopher, scientist, and inventor—did experiments on electricity. Franklin was greatly impressed by a traveling scientific showman from Scotland named Archibald Spencer, who happened to visit Franklin in the summer of 1743 and aroused Franklin's interest and curiosity about electricity. From that time on, for nearly eighty years, scientists experimented on electric current, magnetism, and electric batteries until Michael Faraday, an English physicist, invented the first electric motor and dynamo in the year 1830. From that time on, for nearly two centuries, tremendous advances in the production, transmission, and uses of electrical energy have revolutionized the whole world.

NUCLEAR ENERGY

This is a fascinating new form of energy; the discovery of which is merely sixty years old. This is the energy produced by controlled splitting of the atoms of certain radioactive metals like uranium (U), thorium (Th), and plutonium (Pu). The credit for this discovery goes to British scientist Sir James Chadwick, who discovered in the year 1932 that a form of radiation found by other scientists was really an uncharged particle of the atom with a mass equal to the mass of a proton. He gave this particle the name neutron because it does not carry an electric charge like the electron and proton.

Later scientists who experimented in laboratories bombarded the atoms of uranium with neutrons discovered that the uranium atom was split into two parts, releasing a tremendous amount of heat. This reaction speculated the possibility of a chain reaction analogous to the combustion of wood or coal. In the year 1939, the same year as the start of World War II, American and German scientists succeeded in creating a controlled chain reaction in such materials as uranium, plutonium, and thorium.

Uranium and plutonium can sustain the neutron chain reaction by themselves. However, thorium is a material that, on absorbing neutron from uranium, becomes the fissile material and can also sustain the chain reaction like uranium does. After the end of World War II, further research in nuclear technology of fission led to the building of the world's first nuclear power plant in 1956 at Calder Hall in England. The second was built at Shippingport, Pennsylvania, in 1959.

Within a twenty-year period after the success of these power plants, 415 nuclear power plants were built around the world, mostly in the US, France, and England with an unparalleled safety record. This is the story of nuclear energy, which is widely used in most countries. In the USA, there are two hundred nuclear power plants in operation built between 1960 and 1980.

ENERGY CONVERSION

After the scientific inventions of the last two centuries and the industrial revolution all over the world, Earth's material resources and energy resources have changed people's lives exceedingly. The resources of coal, natural gas, water, oil, and uranium deposits are used to produce electric energy that is converted to run factories, heat and cool the buildings, and light the streets and homes. One form of energy is converted to another form for the optimum use of resources as and where needed.

Innovative methods and technologies are developed to utilize Earth's nonconventional resources such as wind energy and solar heat energy to produce electric power and heat the buildings.

This concludes the learning of a part of the science of creation and the marvelous achievements of dedicated scientists, engineers, and inventors of many generations.

CHAPTER 6

OUR PLANET EARTH
(CONTINUED)

INTERNAL STRUCTURE

A lot more is now known about the internal structure of Earth than was known a century ago. First, the knowledge of the upper surface of Earth is mainly acquired by modern technology of borehole investigations for natural resources such as coal, oil, and gas. At present, boreholes have extended to a depth of two hundred thousand feet below the surface, which is a very small fraction of Earth's diameter of eight thousand miles. Then how can knowledge about Earth's deeper interior be obtained? This is only possible through the most sophisticated modern technology of seismic wave propagation. By the global network of seismic instruments, stations of each country and by the recording of data at various stations, great details are known about the interior regions of Earth than was previously possible. Figure 6.1 shows a cross section of Earth and briefly shows the interior and the representative exterior features, such as oceans, mountains, and dry land surface.

CORE

The innermost part of the earth is called the core. The core is very hot and is composed of molten iron and nickel constantly in motion. The temperature of the core is 6,000°F to 10,000°F and a pressure of 4 million atmospheres. This is a great mystery of creation. The core is also spherical with a diameter of 4,400 miles—just more than half of Earth's diameter. The constant motion of molten iron and nickel and the effect of Earth's spinning about its polar axis is responsible for Earth's magnetic field. The magnetic field of Earth diverts the very dangerous radioactive solar wind away from Earth. This is one of the wonders of divine intervention as stated by the seventeenth-century scientist Isaac Newton. Solar wind is a by-product of thermonuclear fusion going on in the Sun to create heat and light energy.

MANTLE

Above the core is Earth's very hot interior known as mantle with temperatures of 2,000°F to 4,000°F. It has a thickness of 1,800 miles and surrounds the core. The mantle is neither liquid nor solid but is in a plastic state. This is the same material that comes out of active volcanoes in the form of lava and becomes volcanic ash. Volcanology is a special branch of science devoted to the study and investigation of volcanoes. The volcanic materials are studied under the microscope for chemical analysis. Scientific knowledge of Earth's mantle is due to the research and study of the volcanic ash and lava by scientists called volcanologists. There is no other way of reaching this hot material. Other methods of investigations are by seismic waves using sophisticated instruments.

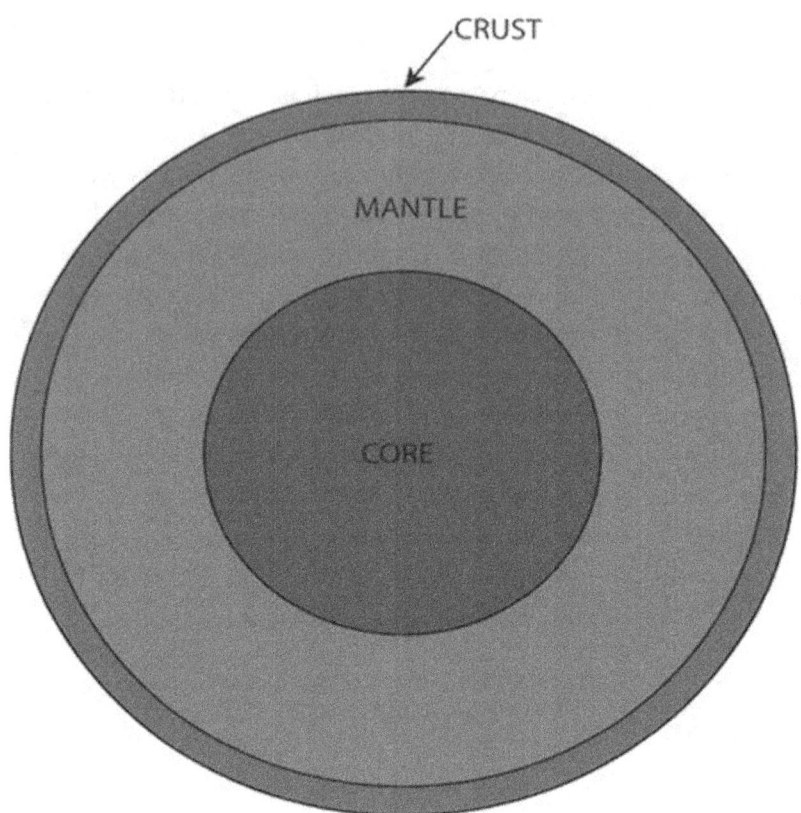

Fig. 6.1 Internal Structure of Earth

CRUST

The top solid part of Earth, on which we live, is called the crust by its scientific name. Average thickness of the crust is eight miles, a tiny fraction of the earth's diameter. However small a fraction this is, it is the most important part for us and to our lives and livelihood. There are two million species of life on Earth—which include animals, plants, birds, insects, and microorganisms—that are dependent on Earth's crust. Wonderfully, the crust contains oceans, rivers, lakes, mountain ranges, deserts, rain forests, glaciers, polar caps among all other things. Earth's crust is one of the wonders of creation and is as beautiful and beneficial as everything else in the universe. The top of Earth's crust was the home, for many generations, of our long-gone ancestors and will be the home of our descendants to come. We study it and everything about it with keen interest. Within the last century of scientific advances, we have known very much in detail about Earth, which we will discuss in the remaining sections of this chapter.

ROCKS AND MINERALS

Earth's crust is made of rocks that contain all the minerals in the form of elements and various compounds of elements. There are about a thousand distinct kinds of minerals known in the rocks, and each mineral has its distinct chemical composition. Rocks are also of many different types structurally arranged in the crust in systematic and surprisingly beautiful patterns. The various groups of rocks include igneous rocks, sedimentary rocks, metamorphic rocks, and organic rocks. A specialty of science devoted to the study and investigation of rocks is called geology.

In addition to rocks, Earth's crust contains sands, gravels, and clays in various proportions. These are the by-products of the weathering of rocks by the actions of water, wind, frost, and chemical decomposition. Therefore, sands and gravels have the same mineral composition as the parent rocks from which these are formed.

Another specialized branch of science that deals with the research and study of minerals is called mineralogy. The study of minerals in the laboratory is a very fascinating occupation. Samples of rocks and minerals are ground so thin and pasted on glass slides. These are then examined through a very high-powered microscope. Each type of mineral displays a very beautiful-colored pattern with magnifications of several thousands.

Minerals are grouped into eight major chemical divisions. These groups are elements, sulfides, chlorides, oxides, sulfates, phosphates, carbonates, and silicates. For example, coal, graphite, and diamond are elements by the name of carbon. Similarly, iron pyrite is iron sulfide; table salt is sodium chloride; quartz is silicon dioxide; and gypsum is calcium sulfate.

SANDS, GRAVELS, AND CLAYS

All sands, gravels, and clays are loosely bound particles of the same minerals as the parent rocks. These cover about three-fourths of dry land surface, and then one-fourth is covered by rocks of various types. Soils are distinguished from sands and gravels because the particles of soil are so small that they can float on water. Also, soils can absorb water by capillary action. Another distinction is that plants and vegetation can grow abundantly in soils, but only rare plants can grow in gravels, sands, and rock ledges. The predominant mineral constituents of soils are silicates and carbonates of calcium and magnesium with some iron and aluminum oxide. Some soils contain more acidic minerals whereas others have more alkaline. Also, soils contain organic matter and bacteria that convert atmospheric nitrogen into plant food for the growth of the plants. Soils contain all the minerals necessary for the growth of plants and vegetation, which provide us food in the form of fruits and vegetables. Thus, the soils—with the help of water and Sun's energy—make the plants, vegetables, and fruits grow. This wonderful network of the Creator will be discussed more in later chapters devoted to life on Earth.

BRANCHES OF EARTH SCIENCES

There are several very specialized branches of Earth sciences, which are listed below:

Geochemistry is a relatively new branch of science devoted purely to the chemistry of the materials of Earth's crust. This branch is highly valuable for departments related to agriculture and forests and many agencies associated with land.

Petrology is a sister science of geology devoted to the study of rocks for exploration of natural resources—coal, oil, and gas—under Earth's surface.

Paleontology is the science of the study of the remains of plants and animals found in geological formations discovered by geologists. Paleontologists can determine the relative ages of rocks by modern methods of carbon dating using the fossil remains of animals and plants.

EARTH'S ATMOSPHERE

Unlike the Moon, Earth has an atmosphere rich in oxygen, nitrogen, hydrogen, and carbon dioxide needed to support animal and plant life. Three-quarters of Earth's surface is covered with waters of oceans and only one quarter is dry land. For water animals and plants, oxygen-rich water and nutrients are ready at hand. However, for land plants and animals, the water has to be transported from the surface of oceans. To accomplish this mighty task, the Almighty Creator has devised a wonderfully efficient system in the form of the atmosphere's weather. Due to the heat of the Sun, changes from one air mass to another in an area along defined lines are called "fronts." Variations from very hot air in tropics such as Central Asia, Africa, mid-USA, and Australia to very cold mass in Siberia, Russia, and Canada cause the movement of air mass that carry with it considerable moisture that causes rain, snow, or hail to dry land. Most of the water gets absorbed by dry land. The excess water overflows to streams and rivers, which will eventually be discharged into lakes and oceans. A small part stays as moisture in the air. Thus, not a drop of precious water is wasted uselessly. This is another wonderful design by the Creator. The branch of science that studies daily weather patterns is called meteorology, and each country has a department to study and forecast daily weather.

HYDROLOGY

When excess rainwater flows over land to streams, rivers, and lakes, the branch of engineering to calculate the amount of water going into each river is called hydrology. Since the amount of overflowing water also depends on the amount of rainfall, the science of meteorology and the engineering of hydrology work side by side. This is to estimate the levels of floods in streams, rivers, and lakes and their daily variations. As water is essential for plants, animals, and humans, the branches of the science of meteorology and the engineering of hydrology are highly developed by modern methods of digital computations to a very high degree of accuracy.

EARTHQUAKES

As perfect and beautiful as our blue planet is and as most suited as it is to all living creatures, occasional ground shaking occurs at certain locations of Earth. Not much was known about these ground shakings called earthquakes until a few decades ago. Modern methods of seismic explorations have discovered that there are big cracks in Earth's crust called faults, in scientific terminology. These faults occur only in certain regions, such as in the West Coast of North America and South America, coastal areas of the Mediterranean, and along the Himalayan mountain range. Possibly due to Earth's rotation or due to thermal changes in Earth's crust, stresses keep building at the locations of these cracks until the stress exceeds the strength capacity of the rock. When this occurs, parts of the rock on either side of the crack shift, causing a tremendous release of energy in the form of earthquake shock waves. These types of earthquakes are predominant and are called tectonic earthquakes; and they cause much damage to buildings, bridges, and other facilities. Another type of earthquake is called volcanic earthquake. This is caused by the eruption of volcanoes and is often localized. These types do not cause much damage, mainly because such areas are thinly populated. The third and least violent of earthquakes is the man-made type caused by the collapse of man-made facilities such as a coal mine or a lake bed.

However frightening the havoc caused by an earthquake is, modern technology of sciences has sufficiently advanced for earthquake-proof construction of all facilities such as bridges, homes, high-rise buildings, underground structures, airports, and in fact, every man-made facility. All these methods and technologies have been acquired within the last few decades of research and investigation in the branches of the science of seismology, geology, geotechnical engineering, structural, civil, electrical, and mechanical engineering. In fact, some critical and sensitive mechanical systems are subjected to shaking-table tests before they are installed. Shaking tables in the laboratory simulate the ground motion of the most severe earthquake ever recorded in the region for which the facility is designed. Thus, the research and investigations of dedicated scientists and engineers during the last several decades helped to mitigate the fear of earthquakes as was not the case a century ago.

BIOSPHERE

This is the region around Earth that extends several feet below the top of dry land, several hundred feet below the top surface of oceans, and several thousand feet of atmosphere above ground surface. It is called biosphere because it supports the abundance of life on Earth.

At several feet below ground surface, no plant or animal life can survive because of high temperatures and lack of nutrients. Again, at several thousand feet in the air, there is a lack of oxygen and warmth for bird life to survive. Similarly, at several hundred feet below the surface of water, hydrostatic pressure is too high for ocean creatures to survive. Thus, biosphere is a very small fraction of the total mass of Earth for supporting life. However small this mass is, it supports an amazing cycle of biological and chemical changes; one ponders with awe and astonishment the intricate balance of life on Earth. This is another marvel of creation that will be discussed in later chapters of this book.

CHAPTER 7

LIFE ON EARTH

PLANTS AND VEGETATION

"Then God said 'Let the Earth sprout vegetation, plants yielding seed, and fruit trees bearing fruit after their kind, with seed in them, on the Earth,' and it was so." NAS Bible

Fossil remains of the life of vegetation origin were first discovered in rocks in the province of Cambria in Wales in Great Britain about two centuries ago. These remains could be of a flower or a tree, preserved in the surrounding rocks either as petrified or chemically transformed bodies of once living vegetation. Because these were first studied in Cambria, the geological age to which they belong is called the Cambrian Period of the Paleozoic group. This is the first stage of life on Earth, so it was named after the place from where it was discovered.

There are 1/3 million species of plants on Earth, which include marine plants. This great variety of plants is a marvel of creation. The largest three-hundred-foot sequoia tree in California and the smallest single-celled microscopic yeast are the marvels of nature, which is the subject of study of the botanist as a scientist. The botanist looks at a plant for what it is: a thing of wonder.

As a living thing, a plant breathes; it grows and it reproduces its exact kind. A plant needs water, soil, and sunlight for its growth. Plants absorb water and minerals from the soil, use energy from the sunlight, and use carbon dioxide from the air to photosynthesize its own food. The leaves have a network of veins like the veins in a human body. These veins are the tiny tubes that carry water and minerals into the leaves, just like human veins carry the flow of blood to parts of the human body.

Plants are the food source of all other creatures on Earth. Botanists are learning a great deal about the life of plants and about life in general from the studies of plants. From these studies, scientists learn about diseases that attack man, such as fungus infections.

Some plants can grow only in certain soils and certain climates. Other plants can grow in all climates. Wheat is such a plant; it can grow in all climates—cold as well as tropics. It can grow in spring, summer, and winter. Wheat is such a blessed plant that its grain contains the complete food nutrients—proteins, minerals, and carbohydrates—necessary for the human body. Wheat is one of the plants that can grow in all the countries inhabited by humans.

PLANT CELLS

In the bodies of plants, there are millions of microscopic organisms called cells. The cells have the marvelous capacity for self-care. A cell keeps itself alive and reproduces. They reproduce and multiply through a process called binary fission. When a cell reproduces itself, it divides and subdivides and so on. This is the process of growth common to all plants and animals. The difference between plant cells and animal cells is that animal cells have a nucleus while plant cells do not. Within the plant cell, the energy from the Sun is absorbed and transformed into the energy of carbohydrate molecules.

This transformation of the Sun's energy takes place only in the cells of the leaves and not in the cells of the roots. Each cell of the plant has a membrane wall around it. This membrane wall is called the plasma membrane, which protects the cells from damage from the external environment. When viewed through a microscope with a magnifying power of several thousand times, the internal structure of a cell is in itself a marvel of creation.

CLASSIFICATION OF PLANTS

Scientists classify or group the plants into categories according to their likeness and differences. These groups are called the species of the plants. To group a plant into a classification according to species, the scientists observe it carefully. They observe all parts of the plant together. They examine the leaves, the roots, the flowers, and the fruits.

Interestingly, some plants do not have roots, stems, flowers, or leaves. Such plants are subdivided into three subgroups: algae, fungi, and lichens. The familiar green scum on the surface of ponds is the algae plant. Botanists and geologists hypothesize that green algae is the first life the Creator breathed into a nonliving molecule, thus ending the long, lifeless era of Earth. Seaweeds and many freshwater algae are visible to the naked eye. However, there are many types of algae that can only be seen through a microscope.

Fungi also have many kinds. Bacteria and cyanobacteria are the most common types of fungi. There are more than a thousand kinds of bacteria. Most bacteria are harmless, such as those in soils. Many types of bacteria are healthy types, such as those in yogurt. Only a few are harmful and are called pathogenic bacteria. Bacteria and cyanobacteria are the most versatile of living species known—some can survive in extreme cold, some in extreme heat, some without oxygen, and some thrive in the presence of oxygen.

Many fungus plants are molds that grow in dark, moist spaces. Molds grow on foods, wood, paper, leather, and many other objects. Fungi differ from other plants in an important way. They cannot make food for themselves. To get their food, fungi attach themselves to other food-making plants, and they help each other for nourishment through a process called mutualism.

Lichens are a sort of combination of algae and fungi. The algae in lichens make food for themselves and also for the fungi. There are many kinds of lichens. They can often grow in places where neither algae nor fungi can grow alone, such as on bare rock ledges, in extreme heat, and in extreme cold.

Ferns are another type of plant that once made most of Earth's vegetation. Fossils of fern leaves are often found in coal seams. Some scientists hypothesize that, long ago, ferns were giant trees and spread across Earth. When they were buried, they formed the modern coal beds under the pressure of the rock strata. This hypothesis does not seem credible because coal is a natural element of Earth just like other elements and is part of rock formations. If this hypothesis were true, natural gas and oil found under the sea should also have decomposed from some other trees. This is not possible under oceans and seas. It is universally accepted that all minerals and hydrocarbons are natural deposits formed at the time our Earth was formed, and so are the coal beds. As will be discussed later, it is not difficult to put forth a hypothesis, but to prove it is not an easy task.

After algae, fungi, lichens, bacteria, and ferns, the most predominant group of plants is the one that has seeds for their reproduction. The seed plants are again two types. One type has flowers and bear covered seeds. Grasses, bushes, and most fruit trees come in this category. Banana tree is an exception. The second type of trees is called evergreen and includes pines, spruces, firs, and hemlocks. Their seeds are found in cones.

CHEMISTRY OF PLANTS

Just like how animals have glands in their bodies to manufacture hormones for their growth, plants have growth hormones important to the roots, stems, and buds. The root of a plant is the underground part, which is made up of cells that do not need sunlight and, therefore, do not photosynthesize the Sun's energy. The roots serve two purposes: first, to hold the plant in upright position and second, to absorb the water and minerals from the soil. There are different kinds of roots in plants. Some are long, like the roots of a dandelion. Other roots spread out in all directions. The roots of most grasses spread in all directions. The roots of big trees go very deep and spread in all directions for moisture and minerals.

Some are root vegetables like beets, carrots, turnips, and radishes, which we eat as part of our diet. The peanut is a very peculiar plant because the seed of a peanut grows at the root.

Interestingly, some plants have male and female species. The female species produce egg cells to be fertilized by the male species. In modern apple orchards, male and female plants are planted in alternate rows for best crop production. Some plants like pine trees produce both male and female cones on the same tree. In spring, the male cone releases pollen, which is blown about by the wind. Some pollen gets trapped on the female cone where it germinates and forms a pollen tube and makes its way into the ovule. The male sperm cell fertilizes the egg, which develops into an embryo within the ovule. In time, the embryo matures to form a seed. Eventually, the seed falls from the cone into the ground, and the germinating embryo becomes a new pine tree.

This explains in a nutshell the life cycle of plants that is very much analogous to the life cycle of animals. Plants, like animals, are living beings and have a definite life span. This is not true for nonliving things.

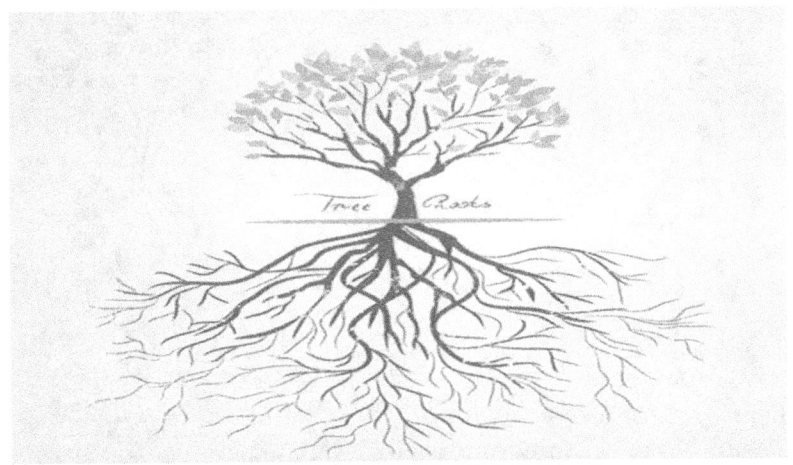

Fig. 7.1 A Typical Tree

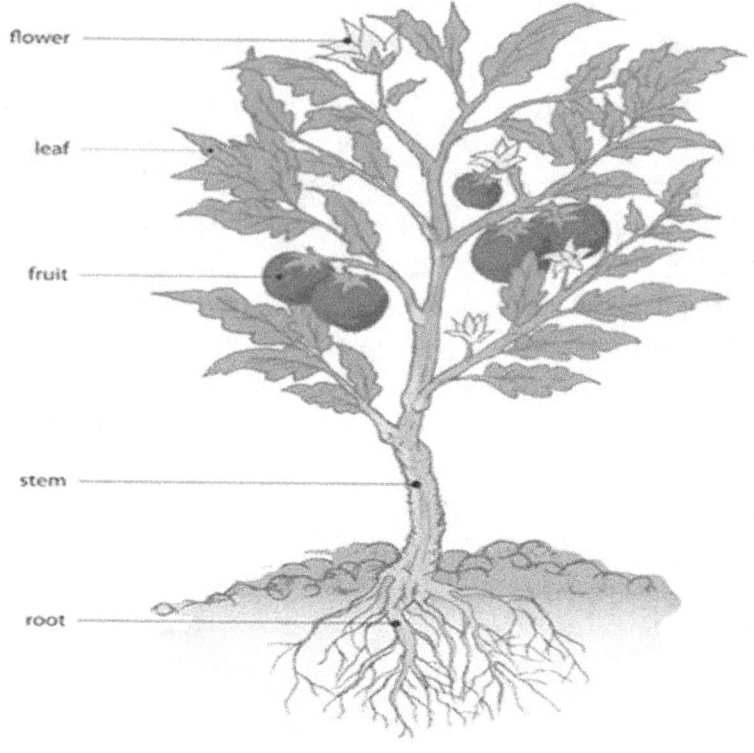

flower

leaf

fruit

stem

root

Fig. 7.2 Fruit Vegetables

Fig. 7.3 Root Vegetables

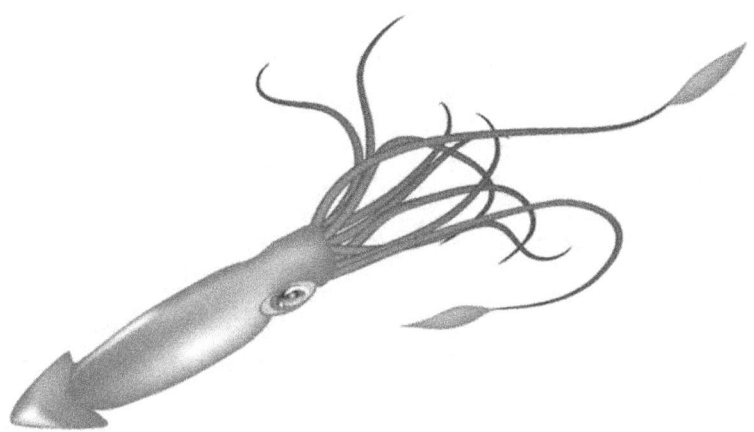

Fig. 7.4 Marine Life

WATER CREATURES

"Then God said 'Let the waters team with the swarms of living creatures, and let birds fly above the Earth in open expanse of the heavens.' And God created the great sea of monsters, and every living creature that moves, with which the waters swarmed after their kinds, and every winged bird after its kind; and God saw that is was good." NAS Bible

This is the second advance of life development on Earth and is called Mesozoic geological age. This group has three divisions in Europe—namely, Triassic, Jurassic, and Cretaceous. The name Jurassic comes from Jura Mountains in France where it was first discovered as fossil remains in rock beds.

LAND ANIMALS

"Then God said, 'Let the Earth bring forth living creatures after their kind; cattle and creeping things and beasts of the Earth after their kind;' and it was so. And God made the beasts of the Earth after their kind and cattle after their kind, and everything that creeps on the Earth after its kind; and God saw that it was good." NAS Bible

This is the third advance of life on Earth and is called the Tertiary Period of the Cenozoic geological age group.

MAN AND WOMAN

"Then God said, 'Let us make man in our image, according to our likeness; and let them rule over the fish of the sea and over the birds of the sky and over the cattle and over all the Earth, and over every creeping thing that creeps on the Earth.' And God created man in his own image, in the image of God he created him, male and female, he created them." NAS Bible

This is the fourth advance of life on Earth called the Quaternary age of the recent and latest geological age group called Holocene. Geologists have discovered remains of bones of human bodies all over the world estimated by carbon dating to be over a million years old.

Among the living creatures on Earth that comprise over a million species, humans are the only one capable of long-term memory and the ability to record the events of the past for future generations. Before the invention of writing, they used to narrate the knowledge of life and history to future generations by word of mouth. Such knowledge was carefully preserved generation after generation. An example of such preserved knowledge is the Vedic hymns of ancient Hindus narrated in Sanskrit language. After the skill of writing was invented, there was still no paper and, therefore, no books were written; knowledge was passed on clay tablets as found in the excavations of the prehistoric towns of Sumer or present-day Iraq and towns of Harappa and Mohenjo-daro or present-day province of Punjab in India and Pakistan. This is the unique attribute of man and woman. That is how the Bible writer has called man and woman: the image of God.

In addition to skills and knowledge of writing, humans possess knowledge in mathematics, science, astronomy, and healing arts, which no other species for billions of years can acquire. With such power of knowledge, man and woman rule over the fish of the sea, the birds of the sky, the cattle all over Earth, and every creeping thing that creeps on Earth.

Another most important attribute that man and woman possess is the knowledge of life and the Holy Spirit—the causative power behind everything that happens. Without the knowledge of science, technology, and the comforts of life, the whole world would have been just a jungle of creatures as it existed for millions of years before man and woman came to rule Earth.

CHAPTER 8

LIFE ON EARTH
(CONTINUED)

The four advancements of life on Earth—namely, vegetation, sea creatures, land creatures, and finally, man and woman—took millions of years to complete. Each species has a definite life span—man's is a hundred years long; dogs, fifteen; horses, twenty; and so on. Total populations of all classes are precisely balanced by the economy of nature. In oceans, planktons are the food source of small creatures, and small creatures serve as food for large creatures, keeping everything in balance.

On land, the situation is slightly different because of climate changes, weather patterns, and influence of man's domestication of animals and plants. In spite of these differences, the populations of plants and animals are also kept in balance by the economy of food sources. The populations become larger if food sources are plentiful and will diminish if food is scarce.

CLASSIFICATION OF LIVING BEINGS

Man and woman, being the rulers of Earth, have studied and researched all life as a scientist does and have learned to classify plants and animals into several classes or families. This is a specialty of biology called taxonomy. One of the earliest taxonomists was a Swedish-born scientist named Carolus Linnaeus who lived in the mid-1700s. Linnaeus published several books and listed thousands of species of plants and animals.

Following the system established by Linnaeus, scientists did further work and published their researches. As the life sciences are very complex, so is the subject of classification of species. With the dedicated effort of scientists over a period of two hundred years, there are 1/3 million species of plants and over a million species of animals presently listed. These are classified in accordance with universally adopted international standard scheme of classification. The first ever published scheme by Linnaeus divided all living beings into two kingdoms—namely, Animalia and Plantae. At that time, microscopic organisms were known but not researched in great detail as is presently done under a microscopic view of several hundred thousand magnifications.

In the year 1860, a German-born scientist named Ernst Haeckel published a scheme of three-kingdom system—namely Animalia, Plantae, and Protista. All microorganisms including fungi and bacteria are listed in kingdom Protista. The current and most updated system of classification was first devised by Robert Whittaker in the year 1968 and is now in use all over the world. This system is based on a five-kingdom scheme—namely (1) Animalia, (2) Plantae, (3) Fungi, (4) Protista, and (5) Monera.

Kingdom Animalia is the largest of all and includes all water and land creatures—birds, fishes, reptiles, worms, and insects. Plantae is the next largest. Kingdoms Fungi,

Protista, and Monera are all microorganisms with several thousand species as discussed in chapter 7.

Other microscopic organisms called viruses are noncellular in nature and lack the properties of living things but have the capability of reproducing themselves inside a living cell. Viruses cause human diseases like pathogenic bacteria. Protection against viral diseases is gained by using vaccine, which is a form of weak or inactive virus to produce antibodies that engulf any virus if it enters the human body until the virus is killed.

ANIMAL KINGDOM

Over a million species of the animal kingdom have been grouped into two major divisions: invertebrates and vertebrates.

Invertebrates are animals that have no backbones, such as earthworms, snails, insects, sponges, squids, etc. This group makes up the larger part of animal species: more than 95% in all.

Vertebrates are animals that have backbones and include fishes, reptiles, birds, and mammals. Both groups are further subdivided into (1) classes, (2) orders, (3) families, (4) genera, (5) species, and (6) varieties.

In accordance with the standard scheme of classification, the definition of a species is that all members of the same species can freely interbreed in nature. Members of different species cannot interbreed, and if forced to interbreed under domestication, their offspring would be sterile. An example is a horse and a donkey of the same genera but different species. When they interbreed, their offspring mule remains sterile.

Again, within the same species, there can be many varieties that can also freely interbreed in nature and under domestication. This topic is of great practical importance in agriculture, horticulture, animal husbandry, and forestry for the production of improved varieties of crops, fruit trees, timber, and domestic cattle. Improved varieties are the result of scientific breeding under controlled conditions for food and other usages. This is the topic of advanced biological research.

INVERTEBRATE ANIMALS

Sponges. Sponges are the most interesting marine animals, and they are hard to distinguish from marine plants. At first, biologists thought they were plants. But after close examination, they found that they were animals.

Sponges have a large central cavity in their body and hundreds of pores in the body's walls. They consume fine food particles through these pores. Cavity walls digest the suspended food particles and water, and they exit the waste through the central opening. Most sponges live attached to rocks, plants, or other animals in marine environments.

Flatworms. These are different from earthworms in that they have organs and a system for digestion, movement, and excretion. They have a system of reproduction in the same body. This is one of the wonders of nature: this animal has male testes and female ovaries in the same body. The exchange of sperm and egg lets the flatworm reproduce itself.

Earthworms. These are very interesting little creatures that absorb their food and water from the soil through their pores in the skin. When needed, water and nutrients are absorbed; the waste passes out of the body also through the pores in the skin. The digestive and circulatory system run the entire length of the body of the earthworm. The earthworm has the unique function, along with bacteria in soil, to convert atmospheric nitrogen into nitrates for plant food for grass and other plants—a wonder of the cycle of life.

Insects. This is the largest group of invertebrates and most highly adapted for every conceivable environment on Earth. They have well-developed organs for smelling, tasting, touching, and hearing. Spiders, ticks, mites, and scorpions have four pair of legs. Grasshoppers, butterflies, beetles, and cockroaches all have three pairs of legs. Some have two pairs of wings. One wonders what purpose these creatures serve. Like earthworms, insects have a great purpose in the economy of nature. Pollination of flowers all happen through the agency of insects without which plant life cannot produce.

Sea Stars and Sea Urchins. These are very interesting sea creatures that have the ability to reproduce by a process called regeneration. A small piece of the animal is able to regenerate itself into an entire body. This is again another wonder of nature. These creatures have a large body cavity and a set of canals inside the cavity.

VERTEBRATE ANIMALS

This division of Animalia has over forty thousand living species. Some of the largest animals to inhabit Earth are vertebrates. Dinosaurs were vertebrates and so is the largest ocean creature, the blue whale. Vertebrates are subdivided into several classes, which are (1) fishes, (2) amphibians, (3) reptiles, (4) birds, and (5) mammals.

Fishes. All fishes are water creatures with a streamlined shape and well-defined tail, which acts as a radar to enable the fish to move rapidly and maneuver through water very cleverly. Some fishes have lungs for breathing, and others breathe through gills in their body. Sharks are one of the species of fish that breathe through gill openings on either side of the throat.

Most fishes living today are bony fishes such as tuna and herring, which live in salt water. Freshwater fishes are trout and goldfish. These fishes have a swim bladder, which is a gas-filled sac to allow fish to change its buoyancy for going deeper or shallower.

Amphibians. Amphibians are creatures that can live in water as well as on land. Frogs, toads, and salamanders are all members of this class. Amphibians breathe air through their lungs and have the ability to breathe through their skin also. They remain in moist environments or in water to avoid dehydration. They lay their eggs in water because the egg would quickly dry out on land. Early stage tadpoles live in water and later come on land as adult amphibians.

Reptiles. Reptiles dominated Earth for millions of years. Modern survivors of the Age of Reptiles are lizards, crocodiles, turtles, alligators, and snakes. Reptiles have well-defined respiratory systems and circulatory systems. Their circulatory system is a three-chambered heart that separates oxygen-rich blood from oxygen-poor blood. Reproduction in reptiles occurs exclusively on land.

Birds. This class of animal has many structural body features that allow them to fly. The body is streamlined to minimize air resistance. The bones are hollow and light. The feathers of birds help in adaptation to flight and are very lightweight. Feathers also insulate the body and help against loss of body heat and water. Birds are able to keep their body temperatures constant by the rapid pumping of blood by their four-chambered hearts and the insulating effect of their feathers. A well-defined tail helps birds to maneuver in flight.

Mammals. The class of animals called Mammalia is distinguished from other classes of animals because they have body hair and nurse their young with milk. There are many families and many species in each family. There are egg-laying mammals that produce milk. Duck-billed platypus, a native of Australia, is an example of an egg-laying mammal.

Other familiar animals in this class are rabbits, deer, dogs, cats, whales, and monkeys. Though humans are a special class in themselves, they fall in the class of mammals in scientific language. Again, in the class of mammals, there are many families. In each family, there are many species. For example, the cat family has the tiger, lion, mountain lion, house cat, wildcat, and so on. Similarly, the monkey class has several families, such as gorillas, chimpanzees, orangutans, apes, and all long-tailed family of primates.

CHAPTER 9

LIFE ON EARTH
(CONTINUED)

THEORIES OF LIFE ON EARTH

LAMARCK'S THEORY

A celebrated French-born scientist named Jean-Baptiste Lamarck put forth a theory in his book published in the early 1800s that species undergo modifications and that all species have descended from some other former species. Lamarck's theory states that species modify due to the following:

1. Changes in physical conditions of life, such as climate or geography.

2. Crossbreeding of different varieties of the same species.

3. Change in habits or instincts of animals.

4. Use and disuse of certain limbs in animals, such the appendix, which in rabbit and grass-eating animals are fully developed and active; whereas, human appendix is useless and ineffective because of disuse.

ERASMUS DARWIN'S HYPOTHESIS

Dr. Erasmus Darwin, the grandfather of famous English-born scientist Charles Darwin, put forth a hypothesis in his book entitled Zoonomia published in 1794. He states that all species including man and woman have evolved from some common ancestors within each class or family. Dr. Erasmus Darwin was a remarkable man of varied interests being a physician, a poet, a philosopher, and a botanist; he was the first to formulate the theory of evolution, which was later elaborated on by his grandson Charles Darwin.

DE VRIES'S THEORY

The theory of Hugo de Vries states that modification of species and, hence, evolution has occurred not by change of habits or physical conditions but because of changes in a germ plasm called mutations. This theory of de Vries's is based on experimentation and laboratory testing under controlled conditions.

DARWIN'S THEORY

Darwin's theory is based on the evolution of new species due to the struggle for the survival of the fittest. The theory of Darwin is summed up in the following statements:

1. The populations of all living beings increase by geometric proportions resulting in intense competition for food.

2. This competition results in such a struggle that new, improved species evolve, which have an advantage over the previous weak species.

3. With the coming of a new stronger species, the old weaker species face extinction whereas the new species flourish.

4. With the passage of time, population further increases, and the process of evolution of new species are repeated and so is the process of extinction of unfit species.

5. The theory of Darwin is founded on three fundamental concepts and publications:

a. Dr. Erasmus Darwin's book entitled Zoonomia published in 1974

b. Thomas Malthus's An Essay on the Principle of Population in which Malthus described the continuous struggle of plants and animals for survival and in which he developed his theory of evolution

c. Sir Charles Lyell's book on the fossil remains of long-extinct species in his publication Principles of Geology in 1830

Darwin's theory further states that innumerable species, genera, and families all descended each within its own class or group from common parents—animals from four or five generations and plants from an equal or lesser number. It is also stated that variations and evolutions occur without any direction and without any design.

PRIMORDIAL SOUP THEORY

In 1953, two scientists named Stanley Miller and Howard Urey performed an experiment in which they circulated methane, ammonia, water vapor, and hydrogen gas in a closed chamber and passed electric sparks through it. After several days, it was discovered that complex compounds of carbon and hydrogen had formed in the chamber. This experiment indicated that in the primitive atmosphere of the earth, complex molecules could form, including amino acids, carbohydrates, and nucleic acids, which are the basis of formation of living cells. It has been observed that living organisms exist in hydrothermal vents deep down in oceans where hot gases and lava emerge from cracks on Earth's crust. Proponents of this theory believe this experiment is a strong point in favor of the primordial soup theory.

MODERN VERSION OF EVOLUTION

Present-day theories of the method of evolution are based on observations and experiments in several fields of biology, such as ecology and population genetics. These theories are based on the Hardy-Weinberg principle, which states that in a certain population of animals where members interbreed at random, the relative proportion of genes remains the same generation after generation. This means that new combinations of existing genes, because of the relative proportions of genes, will remain unchanged. Therefore, for evolutionary change to occur, modifications of gene proportions must occur. The Hardy-Weinberg principle states that for evolution to occur, the following must occur first:

1. Differential mutation occurs if a gene mutation happens more frequently in one direction than back to its original form; the gene proportions change causing tendency to evolve.

2. Gene selection occurs if a mutation gives an advantage to an organism, then it is preserved for natural selection and, hence, evolutionary change.

3. The migration of certain individuals in a population into or out of a given population causes changes in gene proportions, a step toward evolutionary change.

4. A scientist named Sewall Wright has found that in a small population, mutation is more likely than in a large population. Thus, the chance of evolutionary change is more likely in a small population of individuals.

DARWIN'S TRAINING AS A SCIENTIST

Being the son of very successful medical doctor Dr. Robert Darwin and grandson of equally famous and successful medical doctor Dr. Erasmus Darwin of Shrewsbury, England, Charles Darwin was admitted to the school of medicine at the world-famous University of Edinburgh in Scotland in the year 1825 when Charles Darwin was just sixteen years old. In line with family success in the field of medicine, young Charles Darwin was sent to Edinburgh to pursue a medical career. After two years of basic science courses in chemistry, biology, geology, and liberal arts, Charles Darwin told his father that a career as a medical doctor was not for him. With his Christian upbringing, Charles Darwin thought he would do well as a clergy, so his father got him admitted to King's College in Cambridge to study theology. After three more years at Cambridge with several arts, science, theology, and geology courses, Charles Darwin graduated with a bachelor's arts degree in theology to prepare for a career as a clergy. During these five years of college—two at Edinburgh and three at

Cambridge—young Charles Darwin was exposed to many areas of science and met many professors and students. During these five years, his appetite for learning and his serious study habits were greatly enhanced.

DARWIN'S VOYAGE ON THE BEAGLE

Upon graduating with a bachelor's arts degree from Cambridge at the age of twenty-one, young Charles Darwin got the once-in-a-lifetime opportunity to be employed as a royal scientist on the ship HMS Beagle for voyage to remote islands in South America called Galapagos Islands. Darwin's professor and mentor, Sir Charles Lyell, whose book Principles of Geology Charles Darwin studied with interest, advised Darwin to study and record the geology of South America during this trip of five years. Since Charles Darwin was on duty as the only scientist to study, observe, and record his findings in his daily journal, this trip, the job as a scientist, and other personal experiences proved of immense value to Charles Darwin, changing the course of his life from being a village clergy to a world-famous scientist as the father of modern sciences of biology, ecology, and genetics.

After the five-year voyage, the ship returned to England in 1936. Upon returning, Charles Darwin was to write all his observations and findings as a scientist as part of his job. Consequently, he wrote three papers on science, which was published as "Geological Observation," "Zoology of the Voyage of the Beagle," and "An Essay on Origin of Species."

In addition to writing the journals and reports, Charles Darwin was to collect samples of rocks and minerals from various places visited by HMS Beagle . Thus, Charles Darwin, as a royal scientist, was a geologist, a zoologist, and a botanist. He was particularly interested in the coastline of Chile and in the finches and tortoises of the Galapagos Islands.

On returning from the voyage, it took Darwin about two years to complete the journals, give the samples of rocks and minerals for testing to the Geological Society where he met with Sir Charles Lyell many times for professional advice as his mentor.

DARWIN'S EXPERIMENTS

After eight years of service as a scientist with Her Majesty's Government (five years on HMS Beagle and three years in London), writing the voyage journals about collecting samples of rocks, minerals, plants, and animals from various regions in South America, Darwin set up his experiments on plants, insects, small animals, and birds in the comfort of his botanical garden surrounded by domesticated birds and animals. During the time of experimentation, Darwin read his huge pile of notes and journals from the five-year trip on HMS Beagle . Since he was also exposed to sciences of geology, chemistry, and biology at Edinburgh and at Cambridge, Darwin was in touch with other European scientists researching on the same or similar topics. As a member of the scientific society called Linnaean Society of London, Darwin started publishing his essays about his research findings, which got the attention of other European scientists.

DARWIN'S CONCLUSIONS

COMPARATIVE LIMBS

Darwin has offered, as evidence of his theory of natural selection, the comparison of the structure of arms of a human; the forelegs of a horse; the structure of the wings of birds, bats; the flippers porpoise; and the paws of a cat. Darwin suggested that though forelimbs of different animals are used for different purposes—that is, for lifting, walking, and flying—these similarities are common to the ancestor of modern species of birds, bats, humans, porpoises, and cats. He suggested that various modifications are nothing more than adaptations to the special needs of modern species. Though this statement seems more like science fiction than real science, all evolutionary scientists believed in it because it was put forth by such an eminent scientist as Charles Darwin. We will be discussing more about such topics in chapter 10, the final and concluding chapter of this book. Presently, we will just ponder on these statements since the survival of the fittest theory does not have any bearing on this comparison.

EVIDENCE OF FOSSIL RECORDS

Darwin studied the book Principles of Geology by Sir Charles Lyell, which also includes the study of fossil remains of plants and animals that lived millions of years ago. The study of fossil remains of animals and plants in the form of bones, shells, and teeth is a branch of science called paleontology. As paleontologists dig deeper and deeper into layers of rock, the complexity of fossils decrease. As fossils from the uppermost layers of rock are most likely of current species—which are more complex than the fossils from the more ancient, deeper, and simpler species—Darwin speculated that animals and plants fossilized in deeper layers are ancestors of current living species. This is again a conjecture and cannot be proven, like the tests in the real test laboratory. As stated earlier, it is not difficult to put forth a hypothesis, but to prove it requires a lot of scientific testing.

COMPARISON OF EMBRYOS

By observing visually the embryos of many different animals so similar in structure, Darwin believed it as an evidence of common ancestry. Various parts of different animals are exactly alike during the early embryonic stage but become widely different because of widely different purposes in the full-grown adult stage. Darwin quoted Karl Ernst von Baer, another scientist who stated that the embryos of mammals, birds, and lizards in their earliest stages are exceedingly alike so much so that it is possible to distinguish between embryos of various animals only by their size but not by their shapes. This similarity in the embryos of widely different animals is believed by evolutionary scientists to be a proof of common ancestry. Again, this is a matter of belief and conjecture and has no scientific basis.

COMPARISON OF BIOCHEMISTRY

The branches of the science of microbiology and biochemistry were not known in Darwin's times; modern evolutionary scientists profess that conclusions of Darwin had the support of evidences from cell biology and that the chemical systems of all living beings are alike. This refers to the mechanisms of growth by building proteins from amino acids and DNA and RNA mechanisms for inheritance and gene activity. This uniformity of all living beings is advanced as a proof of evolution. This plant will be debated in chapter 10, the concluding chapter of this book.

EVIDENCE OF CONTROLLED BREEDING

For over a period of twenty years, Darwin experimented on plants, animals, insects, and birds and produced new, improved varieties. From the idea of producing varieties domestically, Darwin pondered over the idea that after many generations in nature, the varieties will turn into distinct species and hence, the idea of evolution by natural selection. For example, pigeon fanciers have developed many races of pigeons through domestic breeding. The development of new agricultural crops by farmers and horticulturists point to the development of new species in nature after many generations. This is valid experimental evidence in favor of the development of new species by mutation, but this applies only with families and genre because no experiments have been performed that lasted for generations to create new genres and widely different families.

EVIDENCE OF GEOGRAPHICAL VARIATION

As Darwin traveled to Galapagos Islands and studied finches and tortoises of many species, he found that many species of birds and animals on these islands were only found there and nowhere else in the world. He found that there were thirteen species of finches on these islands and speculated that these thirteen species had evolved from a common ancestor many generations ago. Darwin extended these observed findings to other geographic regions and other species of animals in the formulation of his theory of natural selection. For instance, there are some animals in Australia and New Zealand that are found nowhere else in the world.

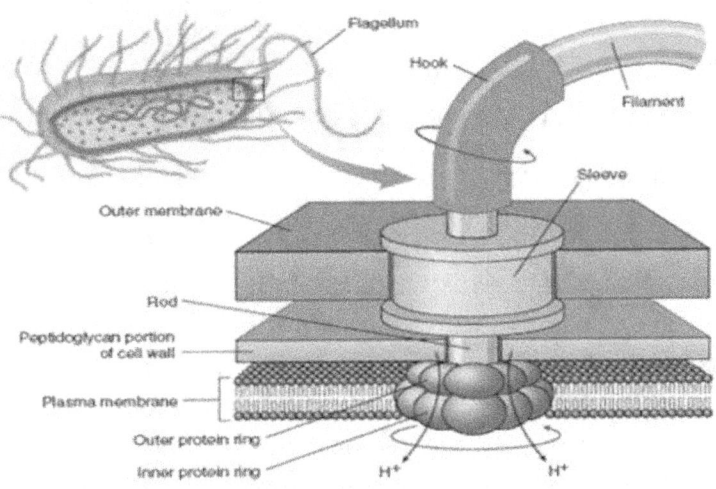

Fig. 9.1 A Single Celled Bacterium

CHAPTER 10

LIFE ON EARTH
(CONCLUDED)

AN OVERVIEW AND CONCLUSIONS

LIFE SCIENCES

The subject of life and life sciences is of an extreme complexity as regards the chemical structure of a living cell, its growth, reproduction, maturing and its decay. When viewed through a microscope of several thousand magnifications, a living cell (Fig 9.1) is a marvel of creation. During Darwin's time of the early 1800s, the science of biology was in its infancy and the specialties of microbiology, biochemistry and genetics were non-existent.

Very rapid strides in the knowledge of life-sciences were made in the nineteenth century by the dedicated efforts of celebrated scientists like Jean-Baptiste de Lamarck, Alfred Russel Wallace, Charles Darwin, W.C. Wells, Asa Gray, Geoffrey Saint-Hilaire and many others.

GEOLOGICAL RESEARCHES

Coincidentally, the knowledge of geology such as sedimentation, rock formations and ages of various rock strata also advanced rapidly in the seventeenth and eighteenth centuries. Along with geology, the study of fossil remains of animals and plants in various rock formations also advanced at the same time. From the study of fossil remains, the four stages of advancement of life on earth as illustrated in Chapter 7 were discovered. These four stages are plant life, marine creatures, land animals and finally, man and woman. Although the geological records are not perfect, the biologists built their theories based on these records. In some cases, a long extinct species re-appeared in a later formation. Various theories such as Lamarck's theory, Primordial Soup Theory and most prevalent Darwin's theory are based on geological records.

BIOLOGICAL RESEARCHES

As the theories of life came into existence, it sets into motion thought process of European and American Scientists for additional researches resulting in rapid advances in the knowledge of life sciences. When the scientists published their findings, some new findings supported their theories and others contradicted them. Because of these contradictions, Darwin's theory of evolution came in for a great deal of criticism by the leading biologists, at times the criticism became so violent that for a period of thirty years from 1895 to 1925 they banned the teaching of Darwin's theory in schools and colleges and banned Darwin's books from state and public libraries.

In view of Darwin's commendable work of researches and usefulness of his findings in the subject of Ecology, Taxonomy and Genetics, leading scientists added modifications to Darwin's original theory giving it a new lease of life.

Because of non-existence of high powered microscopes of magnifications of hundreds of thousands, the subjects of biochemistry and microbiology were unknown in Darwin's time. Whatever theories those dedicated scientists perceived, based on their observations, were commendable. The present day contradictions are as a result of advancement of knowledge of sciences of microbiology, biochemistry, ecology and genetics.

PRINCIPLES OF SCIENCE OF CREATION

1. The Creator of infinite power and infinite wisdom brought into existence inorganic matter of 103 elements of earth, of planets, of sun, moon and galaxies in the vast expanse of the universe.

2. When He chose, out of inorganic matter He brought forth life on earth with its four advancements as described in Chapter 7.

3. What we need to know and understand as scientists is that whatever is created is beautiful and has a purpose and function in the greater scheme of the things and the economy of nature. There is nothing in this vast creation which has no purpose and no function.

4. Each of the one hundred three elements of which the Universe is made in proportions needed for proper function, neither more nor less, has a function in the marvelous working of the Universe. This is true for all plant and animal life. Similarly each part of human and animal bodies is created for a specific purpose to serve the life of the body. No part is without a function or without use.

5. In the economy of nature and the greater scheme of things, there is no such thing as lower forms of life or higher forms as stated by some scientists. Each form works for its intended purpose. Since each species is created for a specific purpose, the question of evolution from a lower form to a higher form has no basis in the science of creation. For instance, earth worms and bacteria in soil help to make nitrates as plant food. Insects help pollination of flowers and birds help transport seeds of fruit trees from one region to another region or other continent.

6. The Creator of the universe of billions of galaxies breathed life into hundreds of thousands of families of species at intervals of time in accordance with the plan of the greater scheme of things. After the creation of life of many species including eight legged, six legged, four legged, two legged and legless forms, new improved species came into being with the extinction of some species in accordance with the principles of modification discovered by Jean-Baptiste de Lamarck.

MYSTERIES OF SCIENCE

All science is mysterious and life sciences are especially so. For instance, it is a wonder how two gases; hydrogen and oxygen, bond together to make life giving water, an entirely different kind of substance. Similarly it is a miracle of science that our sun is millions of miles away from earth, yet it supports all life on earth. Plant life is possible only by the heat and light energy of the sun and all animal life is sustained by plant life.

EPILOGUE

The basics of science is the most important foundation for students to learn at early levels of education. Charles Darwin's theory of evolution first published in 1859, had not been given the status of the law of science like other laws of science universally accepted, but is only considered a speculative hypothesis. Teaching Darwin's theory to mature students at college and graduate level is good for intellectual discussions but is considered out of place for primary school students. State Education Board of the State of Tennessee rightfully banned the teaching of the theory of evolution in state schools in the early 1900s because teaching of contradictory and confusing theories to primary school students creates confusion in young minds instead of inspiration.

Throughout the text writer has carefully set forth the universally accepted principles of science. Students are encouraged to do further reading to derive a greater benefit of the material presented in this book.

Hoping this book serves well the intents and purposes for which it is set forth, to inspire young minds for pursuing advanced studies in the areas of science of their choice. As you discover after reading this book, science is a field to discover the optimum use of the resources of the earth.

BIBLIOGRAPHY

1. Alcamo, I. Edward, "Cliffs Quick Review Biology", Cliff Notes, Inc., Lincoln, Nebraska, 1995.

2. Darwin, Charles, "The Origin of Species", The New American Library of World Literature, Inc., 1958, The Folio Society, London, 2008.

3. Darwin, Charles, "The Descent of Man", The Folio Society, London, 2008.

4. Heimler, Charles H. and Price, Jack, "Focus on Physical Science", Charles E. Merrill Publishing Co., Columbus, Ohio, 1969.

5. Kaufman, William J. III, "Discovering the Universe", W.H. Freeman and Company, New York, NY, 1993.

6. Legget, Robert F., "Geology and Engineering", McGraw-Hill Book Company, New York, NY, 1962.

7. Navarra, John Gabriel and Zafforni, Joseph, "Today's Basic Science", Harper & Row Publishers, Inc., New York, NY, 1963.

8. Ryrie, Caldwell Charles, "The Ryrie Study Bible New American Standard", The Lockman foundation, La Habra, California, 1960, Moody Press, Moody Bible Institute of Chicago, Chicago, Illinois, 1976.

Upcoming books by the same author

PLANET EARTH

AND

THE MODERN WORLD

ANCIENT EMPIRES

AND

MODERN RELIGIONS

RISE, POWER AND DECLINE

OF

MODERN EMPIRES

EUROPEAN RENAISSANCE

AND

VOYAGES OF DISCOVERY